MALE
CHASTITY

EXPLORING DENIAL

L. D. CUB

Copyright © 2021 by L. D. Cub.

ISBN: 979-8-505-26261-0

Book and jacket design by L. D. Cub

Published by Locked Cub Stories

TABLE OF CONTENTS

This started as a small project and grew into a novel. I want to thank everyone that contributed content for its production and to my friends for their proofreading assistance and support.

FORWARD

I have explored chastity and orgasm denial for over six years now at the time of the writing of this text and have been in permanent chastity for five years. I started chronicling my experiences on the social media platform Tumblr before they banned adult content. I have switched to a Twitter account since. In that time, I have received many questions and requests for advice over the years that I felt that putting it all down in one text might be beneficial.

When starting to research this project, I was surprised to find that there is very little detailed information out there for beginners, let alone those that are wanting to expand and grow in their chastity journey. The information that is out there is often sponsored by companies and individuals wanting to make money through advertising as well. It is often also from the point of view of a female-dominated, straight relationship. While there is nothing wrong with this and I embrace the full spectrum of sexuality and joy of living your life, I have written this text from the gay male point of view. My hope is by compiling what I have found in addition to my own experiences and thoughts and those of my followers and friends, that you can get a more complete picture of what to expect, how to get started, and address common questions as well.

As such, it is important to reiterate that these are my views and experiences taken from my journey exploring chastity and orgasm denial and permanent chastity. I have also included the point of view of medical professionals as well. I want to make it clear, though, that I do not have a health care or medical background or degree. Additionally, chastity devices are considered sex toys and are not regulated by any country. If you choose to pursue male chastity, you must understand the risks and take responsibility for them. Having said this, I hope you will find this information useful as you explore and start your chastity journey.

CHAPTER ONE

Locked Biology – The Health and Safety of Chastity

Genital Structure and Function

Any discussion of chastity should start with a description of the male reproductive system. This is because many different parts can be affected by chastity and orgasm denial. It is also important to know your body and understand how to avoid issues that may cause temporary or permanent damage. The material presented here in this chapter was collected from publications from a board-certified urologist in Washington State, medical journals, and associated scholarly research.

External Organs

Most of the structure of the male reproductive system is located outside of the male body, which is in contrast to the female reproductive system. The external structures include the penis, the scrotum, and the testicles.

The penis is what a functioning male uses for urination and sexual intercourse. In its flaccid state, the average male penis is on average 3.61 in (9.16 cm) in length and 3.66 in (9.31 cm) in girth. It consists of the root, which is firmly attached to the wall of the abdomen, the shaft, which extends outside of the body, and the glans or head of the penis that is covered by a loose layer of skin called the foreskin.

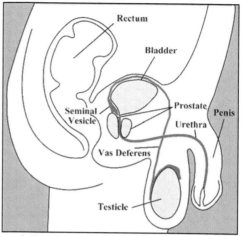

The shaft of the penis contains three internal chambers that are made of spongy erectile tissue. When a male is aroused, these tissues become engorged with blood and expand leading to an erection. In its erect state, the average male penis is approximately 5.16 in (13.12 cm) long and 4.59 in (11.66 cm) in girth.

The head contains several sensitive nerve endings, mostly contained within the foreskin tissue. When removed through circumcision, as is common practice in the United States, a majority of this sensitivity is lost and the skin on the head becomes thicker and tougher than on an intact male. The head also contains the opening of the urethra, the tube that transports semen and urine.

The scrotum, also known as the ball sack, is a loose pouch-like sack of skin that hangs behind the penis. Contained within the scrotum are the testicles as well as many nerves and blood vessels. The scrotum serves a protective purpose for the testicles and acts as a climate control mechanism to promote fertile sperm production. Sperm cells are created within the testicles and they require a specific range of temperatures that is slightly lower than body temperature to function properly. Special muscles that exist in the wall of the scrotum allow for it to tighten and relax and move the testicles closer to or farther away from the body to maintain optimum temperature.

There is wide variability in appearance and function of the scrotal sack among males. Some males find that their scrotal tissues can expand and "hang" relatively low below the body, while others have very little extension at all. This tissue can be trained to expand and permanently extend leading to lower hanging testicles using ball stretching devices. This will be discussed later in chapter two.

The testicles of a male are oval structures 1.5 x 1 x 0.75 in (4 x 3 x 2 cm) in size and lie in the scrotum attached to a structure called the spermatic cord. It is common for one testicle to be a different size than the other. Their primary responsibility is to produce testosterone, the male sex hormone, and sperm. Within these structures are coiled masses of tubes called seminiferous tubules. They are responsible for the production of sperm at a rate of several million per day.

Finally, the epididymis is a long, coiled tube that sits on the back of each testicle and functions as the storage space for sperm produced. Within this structure, the sperm become mature. When a male is aroused and reaches orgasm, contractions force the sperm from the epididymis up through the vas deferens where they are then combined with fluids from the prostate gland and then expelled through the urethra.

Internal Organs

The internal organs of the male reproductive system include the vas deferens, urethra, seminal vesicles, ejaculatory ducts, prostate gland, and Cowper's glands.

As mentioned previously, the vas deferens is a long, muscular tube that travels from the epididymis on the testicles into the pelvic cavity and just behind the bladder. Its primary function is to deliver sperm to the urethra.

The urethra is the main tube that carries urine from the bladder to the outside of the body. In males, it also serves the function of carrying a combination of sperm and prostate fluids known as semen, ejaculate, or cum when a male achieves orgasm. When the penis is erect, the flow of urine is constricted and blocked to allow only the ejaculatory fluids to be expelled.

The seminal vesicles are sac-like pouches that attach to the vas deferens near the base of the bladder. It is in this structure that a sugar-rich fluid (fructose) is produced that provides the sperm with a source of energy and helps with their mobility. It is the fructose fluid that makes up most of the volume of a male's ejaculate and causes it to be white.

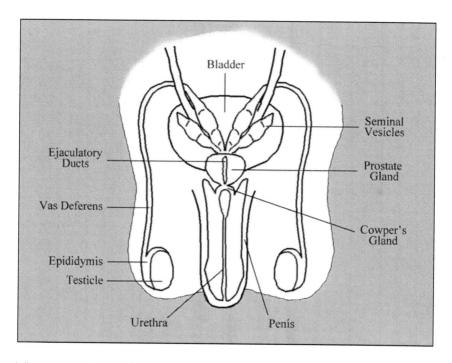

The prostate gland is a walnut-sized structure that lies below the bladder and in front of the rectum. The prostate also produces and stores fluids, which are milky in appearance, which help to nourish the sperm. Research suggests the gland should be emptied regularly to maintain healthy prostate function. The urethra, which carries the ejaculate expelled during orgasm, runs through the center of the prostate.

The ejaculatory ducts function to transmit semen from the vas deferens and the seminal vesicles into the urethra through the prostate gland. They gather all the fluids produced, including prostate fluids, and force them on through the urethra.

Finally, the Cowper's glands are pea-sized structures that lie on either side of the urethra below the prostate. The glands produce a clear, slippery fluid that serves as lubrication for the urethra which is also known colloquially as "precum". Many males have overactive

Cowper's glands and can produce a large amount of precum both before, during, and after ejaculation. Additionally, supplements such as L-Arginine, Magnesium, and Zinc have purportedly been found to increase the production of precum as well.

Normal Function

Hormones are what drive the male reproductive system and these chemicals stimulate and/or regulate the activity of cells and organs. The primary hormones that are involved in the system are the follicle-stimulating hormone (FSH), luteinizing hormone (LH), and testosterone.

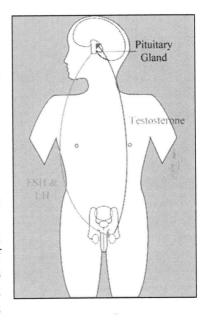

FSH and LH are produced in the brain within the pituitary gland. FSH is used for sperm production and LH stimulates the production of testosterone. Testosterone, itself, is produced within the testicles and drives male characteristics such as muscle mass, strength, fat distribution, bone mass, secondary characteristics (body hair, lower voice, and longer facial features), and the sex drive.

These chemicals are at their highest production during puberty and wane over the lifetime of a male. While males do not go through menopause like females, by the age of forty, the functioning of the testicles decline, and the corresponding production of testosterone drops as well. This can affect the libido of a male and his ability to produce sperm as well.

If testosterone levels fall too low, hormone replacement therapy can be used to stabilize hormone levels within the body, so libido is maintained. Low testosterone can also lead to bone loss and other adverse health effects, which is why males over forty are encouraged to get checked by their physicians regularly.

Males in chastity and orgasm control often will find that their testosterone levels increase in the days and weeks after starting chastity. This can lead to a stronger sex drive and increased sexual urges which can present a large obstacle, especially to those new to chastity. Learning to cope with and control these feelings and sensations is key to success. I will discuss some techniques I have found to be effective to maintain a chaste lifestyle in Chapter Three.

Fluids Produced

Most males are familiar with the ejaculatory fluids known as semen or cum. This fluid is expelled during orgasm and is milky white in appearance and can contain millions of sperm. The average male expels 0.75 tsp (3.7 ml) of cum but it is made of several fluids that have been described previously. The main components are the precum from the Cowper's gland, prostate fluids, seminal fluids, and the sperm itself.

It is the prostate gland that is the concern of most medical practitioners when they hear a male is considering orgasm denial through chastity. Urologists note that the body has built-in mechanisms to maintain the health of its organs. For the prostate gland, which produces and stores fluids used during ejaculation, these fluids must be regularly expelled. Thus, most males will experience nocturnal erections and emissions known as "wet dreams" if they are not ejaculating enough. This action allows the prostate to drain and prevent a build-up of fluids.

The prostate is also a muscular gland. Thus, it is also imperative that it be used regularly to maintain the health of the organ and prevent its weakening. During orgasm, the prostate muscles contract and force prostate fluids into the urethra in combination with sperm, seminal fluids, and pre-cum. However, males in chastity perform orgasm denial, so this does not occur. Additionally, wearing a chastity device prevents normal erections and makes nocturnal emissions more difficult.

While there is little research that has been conducted on long-term orgasm denial or infrequent ejaculation on the tolerance of the prostate, urologists agree that less use has the slight possibility of leading to an inflammation of the prostate, bacterial infections, and weakening of the organ. Thus, it is a good idea for males that are in chastity and practicing orgasm denial to drain their prostate regularly. This can be done through a process called "milking the prostate".

Milking the Prostate

If you perform any search of the internet or social media surrounding chastity and orgasm denial, you will run across someone who mentions they were milking their prostate or had an internal orgasm. Both terms relate to the process of manually manipulating the prostate organ and any male in short- or long-term chastity and orgasm denial should understand this process.

The process of "milking" the prostate allows for the organ to drain and, in the process, release stored fluids. It also will exercise the muscles of the organ to maintain proper health as well. The technique is simple to learn but is often confused with orgasm. When done properly, milking does not involve orgasm and the types of fluids released will appear different than normal semen or cum.

As mentioned previously, the prostate sits between the rectum and the bladder. It can therefore be reached and stimulated through the rectal canal using a finger or external device. The aim is to locate the walnut-sized organ and to rub gently in circular movements. This

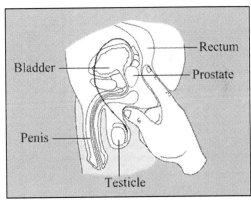

will induce the organ to contract and release the built-up and stored fluids. The sensation for the chaste male can be varied. Many note that it feels as though you need to urinate, others find a warm and pleasurable sensation that emanates from the area. Since this is not connected to full ejaculatory orgasm, the fluids that are released normally do not contain much sperm or seminal fluids, thus usually the fluids that are expelled look cloudy or diluted from normal semen or cum. Additionally, the fluids will often slowly leak out over time and it can take many minutes to fully drain the prostate.

However, caution should be noted when using this milking technique and it must be done carefully. Too much pressure can cause urination and can also lead to full orgasm as well, which is often contrary to what males practicing chastity with orgasm denial desire. It is this full orgasm that many males will mention as an internal or "assgasm". This can be achieved in normal sexual intercourse as well when the penis of a dominant hits this area and induces orgasm.

Blue Balls

At this point, it would be prudent to discuss the phenomena known as "blue balls" as it relates to chastity and orgasm denial and how milking can be used as a relief. Blue balls is a figure of speech to describe a real medical condition known as epididymal hypertension (EH). This is an uncomfortable condition that results from either having an erection for a prolonged period without ejaculation, or in the case of a male in chastity, being aroused for a long period with swelling in the device due to attempted erections and no orgasm.

The penis and testicles contain thousands of blood vessels that expand and fill with blood during an erection. When an erection occurs, the penis stiffens, but the testicles also increase a bit in size as well. After orgasm (or a decline in arousal), the blood normally flows back into the body.

But when that excess blood stays in the genitals for a long time without being released, that increased blood pressure (the "hypertension" in the medical term) can get painful, leading to an ache in the testicles not-so-fondly known as blue balls. This can happen during sexual activity with a partner or an extended masturbation session (edging) without ejaculating or in the case of a male in chastity, denial, or inability to orgasm.

Some of the symptoms of blue balls include a perceived heaviness in the balls or scrotum, an aching sensation, some mild discomfort in the testicles, and even a bit of a faint blue tint in the scrotum, which is likely where the term originated.

Interestingly, the first peer-reviewed paper on blue balls wasn't published until October 2000. The researchers theorized that it's caused by blood flowing into the genitals and not flowing out, leading to swelling, particularly in the epididymis (the tubes behind the testicles, which store and transport sperm). Medical doctors conjectured that if the condition persists and testicular venous drainage is slowed, pressure builds and causes pain. The paper went on to question if epididymal distension was the cause of the pain. As with any condition, there is a wide spectrum of symptoms and degrees of severity depending on the person, varying from brief, mild discomfort to severe, sustained pain.

Medical doctors agree, however, that blue balls are not dangerous. While it can feel distressing and can be a test for anyone in short- or long-term chastity, it is a common and innocuous condition that can be resolved through either orgasm or prostate milking for the male in chastity. Additionally, they note that any bluish hue is subtle and very rare.

Thus, since those in chastity often are also practicing orgasm denial, manipulation of the prostate through the process of milking can allow not only the prostate to drain, but the blood flow to return to the body as well. Chaste males often report that after a milking session, the sensation is often alleviated, and the overall horniness level of a male can be reduced as well.

Medical Advice on Chastity

Erectile Tissue Health

One question many males have concerning long-term chastity is the effect on the erectile tissues of the shaft. As mentioned previously, the shaft contains sponge-like structures that fill with blood to allow the penis to achieve an erection. A well-fitting chastity device will inhibit or prevent a full erection from occurring.

While no long-term medical studies have been done on those that are in long-term chastity, doctors say their primary concern is the long-term health and preservation of erectile tissue. Dr. Stephen King, a urologist in Washington State, notes that poor-fitting devices that put significant compression on the tissue or allow for partial erections that can lead to bends in the shaft could cause damage. However, he notes that custom-fitted devices or those that are properly measured and installed, can support the genitals, and put far less compression on the tissues.

He further states that if there is no compression from the device ring, or the penile tissue is not in a state of extreme compression from being placed in a space that is too small, then the device would be safe for longer use.

Dr. King did note that overnight use may still be problematic. Nocturnal/spontaneous erections are hypothesized to exist to encourage blood flow and stretching of the vascular and erectile tissue to keep it healthy and prevent atrophy. Like any other tendon, ligament, or muscle in the body, you use it, or you lose it. However, having stated this, he says he does not personally see any health issues with preventing these spontaneous nocturnal erections and he can't point to any research showing that long-term damage can result.

It should be noted that there are no cases that have been published where an individual has claimed that a chastity device has caused long-term damage to the penis or been responsible for a loss of sexual function. Additionally, physicians that deal with trauma have stated that there are no known cases that specifically involved chastity or orgasm denial.

So, what happens to the erectile tissues when you wear a chastity device for long periods? As stated, a properly fitting device will limit or inhibit full erections. While the tissues will swell within the confines of the device and back toward the root behind the device ring, they will not achieve the level of blood flow that an unlocked penis will achieve. Over time, the tissues will shrink due to a loss of constant nightly erections.

I have noted that over the time that I have been in permanent chastity, flaccid shaft length and girth has decreased by approximately 35-40%. Other chastity wearers have noted that when removed, their erections are not as firm, and length and girth are reduced. This is a temporary phenomenon, though. Once a chastity device is removed and normal erections are resumed, the tissues will begin to return to normal, though some long-term chastity males have noted that it can take several days to weeks for this to occur.

Because of this atrophy of the tissues, many long-term chastity users must invest in smaller chastity devices over time. Thus, it is important to monitor your device for proper fit and make changes to the length and ring size as needed.

Scrotum and Testicles

Another concern that some doctors have with ball trap chastity devices is the effect on the scrotum and testicles. Ball trap devices use a base ring that surrounds the testicles and shaft and sits flush against the lower abdomen. Poor-fitting rings are the most common cause for discomfort, pain, and damage to not only the shaft of the penis but the testicles and scrotum as well.

If the ring size is not correct, blood flow can be constricted to the scrotum and testicles and they can take on a blue appearance. The device should be immediately removed if this occurs. Long-term use can lead to permanent damage to the testicle or even testicle death. Torsion of the testicles can also occur with a poorly fitting ring as well which requires immediate medical attention.

When a ring is too large, it can allow the device to slip away from the body. This can lead to irritation of the scrotum and sores can develop. Additionally, the shaft can swell during erections and can be bent, which could cause damage to the tissues. If you notice consistent redness or sores on the shaft of your penis while in chastity or underneath the base ring, then you may need to resize your device. If a larger ring is necessary for any reason, a support strap can assist in keeping the chastity device flush against the body and avoiding tissue damage. This type of accessory is described in Chapter Two.

Orgasm Denial

Despite what you may read online or hear from others, orgasm control and denial is not harmful. Many males practice a technique called edging where they bring themselves to the brink, or edge, or climax, and then back off. They then repeat the procedure as many times as they want until they orgasm or put off orgasm. This often can result in the blue balls feeling mentioned previously, but there is no harm done to the system as a whole.

For those in chastity, orgasm control usually is part of the process. Many males that are in chastity will put off orgasm for hours, days, weeks, months, and years. Others will set goals only to have internal orgasms infrequently. Ruined orgasms are also quite frequently associated with chastity as well.

A ruined orgasm is where a male is brought over the edge but before the full climax. This has the effect of leaving the male sexually frustrated and can have emotional effects as well. This is what happens in the cycle of a ruined orgasm:

1. During arousal, blood flow is increased to the genitals leading to an erection and slight enlargement of the testicles.
2. Repeated stimulation leads to a nervous system discharge causing climax and ejaculation.
3. When a ruined orgasm occurs, the male is brought to just before the nervous system discharges and all stimulation is stopped.
4. The male experiences ejaculation but no orgasm occurs.

As with the prostate milking technique mentioned before, this has the effect of allowing the reproductive system to release stored fluids and can be part of keeping a male healthy. Additionally, because the male is brought to the brink and not allowed an orgasm, the chemicals in the brain are never fully released to induce pleasure and a high level of arousal and an accompanying level of frustration is often is maintained. Males in chastity must find ways to cope with these feelings to be successful.

When to See a Doctor

Males practicing chastity and orgasm denial are often resistant to discuss this with their doctor. There can be shame involved or an unwillingness to discuss the practice with an outsider. However, it is encouraged that you discuss this with your doctor, especially if you are considering chastity and orgasm denial for long periods.

Additionally, it is also important to know your body and be aware when changes occur that might require medical attention.

Doctors recommend that you check your device regularly every morning and evening. You should inspect around the ring first to determine if any irritations are showing up or sores developing. It can often be helpful to have assistance with this, so if you have a dominant or keyholder available that can help you check regularly, this can be beneficial. Additionally, if your shaft is being bent or pushing out of the chastity device and you experience any sort of pain, discoloration of the skin, or irritation, you may need to remove the chastity device for some time. If the condition does not improve, then medical attention may be needed.

If you notice any sign of blood, you should immediately remove the device and clean the area with alcohol and apply an antibacterial cream. The device should not be reinstalled until the area has completely healed or more trauma can result.

Another common issue is a chastity device that is not correctly fitted for you. One that is too small a diameter can cause too much pressure on your shaft and lead to edema in the normal process of erectile tissue expansion. A chastity device that has a diameter too wide can allow too much blood to enter the shaft which can then not escape easily. A chastity device too short can also cause too much pressure on the shaft and often lead to a forcing of the chastity device forward and erectile tissue expanding behind the ring. Too long of a chastity device can allow the shaft to expand too much during erection and irritation and sores can develop.

One common solution to reduce these problems is to ensure you have a correctly fitted device, are conducting proper hygiene on your chastity device and body, and are using lubrication where needed. These techniques will be discussed in Chapter Two.

CHAPTER TWO

Beginner's Guide – How to Get Started in Chastity

Chastity Device Basics

Many males can be overwhelmed when they start researching chastity. There are so many different versions of devices that have been produced that I find that where to start and what to start with are two of the most common questions that I receive. In an attempt to help answer this question, I will break down the types of chastity devices into three broad categories and then discuss the variations, pros, cons, and cost involved for each.

History of Chastity

Chastity has been around for a very long time. Like most of our BDSM practices, it likely originated from the medieval and Victorian eras. Chastity devices were most typically associated with females throughout most of history, an idea that stemmed from the social roles of males and females when females more often than not suffered from oppression. The classic example is the medieval lord locking up his wife securely before going off to war to prevent another male from diluting the bloodline.

While such devices did exist, many of the tales and illustrations you see and read about are more sensationalism and gratuitous material to entertain. Indeed, more recent scholarly research has thrown a great deal of doubt on the true history and use of chastity devices and when they became popular. So, the question now becomes, if they didn't exist in medieval times, where has the chastity belt come from?

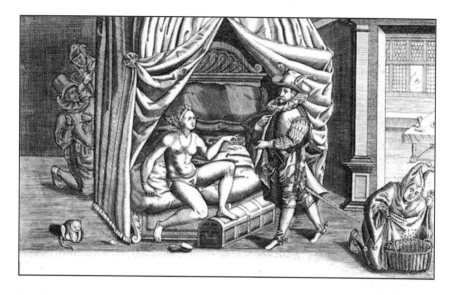

In the British Medical Journal, Lesley Smith wrote an article in 2007 which stated that she has extensively traveled the world and examined a variety of art collections and historical pieces, and she has yet to have seen a chastity belt that can conclusively be proven to have originated from the Medieval period. Smith also believes that the 'joke' stuck because the concept is understandable given the context of social beliefs concerning sex and sexuality at the time. Medieval Europe was a period in which any form of sexual activity that was not related to conception was a sin and ultimately forbidden. A chastity device fits into this contextual belief which has resulted in historians, researchers, and studies concerning the chastity device, to fail to notice the allegorical and satirical humor behind the device, instead of resulting in the proclamation that the chastity device was real.

There is some evidence, however, that the Romans experimented with various types of chastity devices or implements. A bride in Rome, for instance, would often wear a corded belt to indicate they were chaste, and it would only later be taken off by the husband. Perhaps this is where the later ideas of a chastity belt originated as we moved into the middle ages.

The once fabric corded belt could have evolved into a belt ornately designed with metal to symbolize chastity and to separate the idea between the working class (fabric belt) and the upper class (metal belt). This belt was worn around the hips, as opposed to around the female genitals. Most of the historians concerning female chastity devices continually refer back to the same point; that the idea of a chastity device had intended to be a joke, and a failure to acknowledge this is seen as being consistent with a practice with in which modern historians and researchers partook in to conjure a more 'barbaric' version of medieval society than what had existed in truth.

Regardless of whether you subscribe to the idea that chastity devices are a great joke, or whether you believe that they originated from Ancient Roman customs, or even if you believe that they have existed and that historians have attempted to cover up a great sex joke, one cannot deny that they have ultimately morphed into a popular sexual fetish. Though it wasn't until the introduction of the world-wide-web that these devices became more popular to zest up a sexual relationship.

Chastity devices today are a common implement to avoid masturbation as well as denying or reducing sexual activity to anyone other than the key holder to the device. Male chastity devices all have two things in common; the first being that they are designed to prevent an erection. They do this by either having a short tube that encases a flaccid penis, or (especially useful for those with large flaccid penises) a curved piece whereby the curve is sharp enough that an erection is impossible. Second, they are designed to be locked up by the key holder or their partner to prevent tampering.

Today, there are so many different types, styles, and variations of chastity devices that it can be overwhelming for those getting started or even for those that are experienced and looking for a new or better device. I will describe some of the most common devices and give my impression of their pros and cons, but I am by no means an expert on all devices, so I will rely on some internet reviews as well.

Ball-Trap Devices

The most common and cheapest types of male chastity devices are ball-trap devices. These devices rely on a rigid or hinged ring that surrounds the balls and shaft and sits against the abdomen as an anchor for the device itself. It is a cock ring that has a tube attached to it.

The base ring is worn at the base of the penis, situated between the body and the testicles. A tube is then slipped over the shaft and attached to the top of the base ring, forming a small gap between the ring on one side and the bottom of the tube on the other through which the scrotum passes, allowing the testicles to dangle comfortably below. The two parts are then locked together using either a normal padlock or a type of integrated lock or screw.

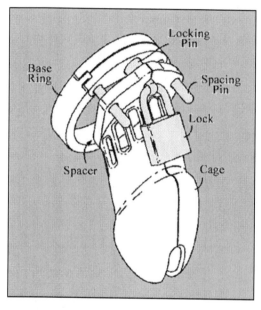

Once locked in place, the wearer's testicles are on the wrong side of a gap that's ideally too small for them to pass through, preventing the device from being removed without being unlocked first. As a result, the penis is imprisoned in the tube, which may be a completely solid or a more open, ventilated design. Either way, a hole or gap at the end allows urine to pass, but it and any other air vents are often too small for a finger to enter, keeping the wearer from fully touching, let alone stimulating his penis without first being released.

There are many variations in this basic style. Rather than having a separate ring and tube, some feature a one-piece design with a handcuff that fastens behind the testicles. Others come with a range of different-sized rings and spacers to allow the fit to be tailored to the individual wearer. Often, they are made from rigid plastic, usually clear although occasionally colored, but metal versions are also available, either stainless steel or chrome plated.

Most chastity devices are "one size fits all" products, readily available "off the shelf" from a range of suppliers at a modest cost. Their unobtrusive design is easily hidden under clothing, and the lightweight plastic of most models is far from burdensome. However, if you are a male like me that needs a large diameter ring to comfortably fit around the balls and shaft, then you can have some issues as most off-the-shelf devices come with, at most, only three to five standard sizes. Thankfully, there are custom options out there that will not break the bank.

3-D printing has come a long way and now offers those interested in low-cost ball-trap devices the option to have a custom device. I have used the company Shapeways to order several 3-D printed devices called the "Cherry Keeper" by Josielynn. An internet search should allow 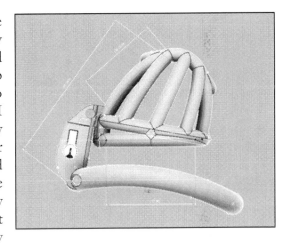 you to find these devices. However, there is a wide range out there. For new males into chastity, these are also a good option since if you measure wrong, you can just order another ring or tube and not break the bank. You can also often get a wide variety of colors as well. Just be sure to get a premium version of the plastic for your tube portion and not the cheaper, standard grade of plastic that is offered.

The ball-trap design relies on the scrotum being loose enough to pass through the gap between the two parts of the device, which can be problematic for males whose balls hang particularly close to the body, especially in cold weather. Moreover, since only the testicles are trapped, this kind of device isn't as secure as the more traditional chastity belt as some males can pull their shaft out of the tube entirely.

19

How difficult this is depends on the individual and the device in question and reinserting it afterward can prove rather more of a challenge. A properly fitting device usually prevents these issues.

PA Piercing Devices

A variation of the ball trap device is the PA piercing device. A Prince Albert or PA piercing is one in which a ring is inserted through the urethra and through either the top or bottom of the glans of the penis. For those with this type of piercing, there are devices that are designed to utilize this and forgo the base ring. For males that have trouble getting a base ring to work comfortably due to a variety of issues, this is sometimes used as a solution.

One variation on the device uses an integrated ring that fits through the piercing with the tube attached to it that sits on the shaft. While this type of device allows erections to occur more easily, the tube portion covers the shaft and 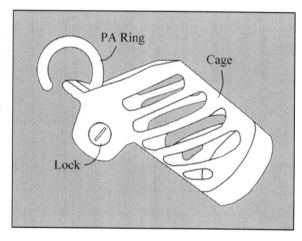 helps to prevent stimulation. This design is not as secure in terms of preventing orgasm, though.

Another variation is to use the traditional ball-trap device with an integrated ring that fits through the PA piercing as well. This offers enhanced security as it is impossible to remove the penis once it is in the device. One must take care with these devices, however, that the ring is properly sized and will not tear the piercing in any way. Additional care must be taken with hygiene with this type of device as well to avoid any infections around the PA ring.

Full Belt Devices

Just as a regular belt keeps a male's pants up, a traditional chastity belt can fasten likewise, relying on his hips being wider than his waist to prevent it from being removed. The wearer's penis is inserted into a tube that attaches to the

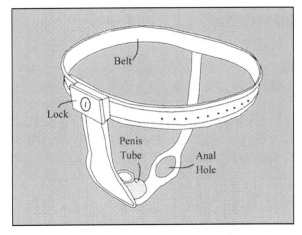

main band of the belt at the front, resting snugly against the body and preventing any access. The base of the tube is held in place by a chain or piece of metal that passes between the buttocks before attaching to the rear of the belt. Once everything is fastened in place, the belt can be locked closed, either with a padlock or a more integrated mechanism.

Again, there are variations. The main band of the belt rests just above the hips in some models, and around the waist itself in others. There may be two chains that pass over the buttocks rather than one between them for increased hygiene, or there may be a wider band with an appropriately placed opening to allow for defecation. The front of the belt may be designed to give a smooth, feminine appearance and both the tube and the belt itself may have special linings to allow longer, more comfortable wear. Finally, some manufacturers offer a wide range of accessories to allow the wearer to attach dildos, for instance, to pleasure their partner while still wearing the belt.

These belts are usually custom-made by individual suppliers and thus are tailored to the precise measurements of the wearer. Generally constructed of metal, they are bulkier and significantly more expensive than their cheaper plastic alternatives, but correspondingly more secure. When correctly fitted, the penis is completely inaccessible and it's impossible to remove the belt without the key unless you're prepared to resort to using heavy-duty equipment. The sturdier design does require more getting used to, however, and wearing one long-term pose certain hygiene challenges, particularly at the rear.

Fitting for a Chastity Device

There are many ways that manufacturers and websites give for measuring for a chastity device. I have found that Lock the Cock (2018) provides one of the best-detailed explanations and I summarize their method here. They also are a great place to start when you are looking for your first chastity device.

Selecting a perfectly sized chastity device is an art. The ideal device will be tight but not painful, constricting, and humiliating but not to the point of physical discomfort, and be able to consistently prevent erection without permanently cutting off blood flow to the penis.

A properly fitted chastity device, if it is kept clean and regularly inspected, can be safely worn round-the-clock without any damage to the penis occurring. It will prevent all typical functions, save for urination, while the penis is enclosed, but ejaculation and even erection will still be possible during rare breaks when the dominant or keyholder allows the subordinate male to be freed.

In particular, measuring yourself and becoming aware of the size and dimensions of your penis (or your partner's penis, if you plan to surprise him with a nice new chastity device) will turn device shopping from a frustrating chore into a simple and even pleasurable activity. This guide will walk you through the process of measuring the penis and sizing a device from the safety and comfort of your home.

First, it is important to understand that a chastity device is not one single, unbroken item. Most devices are ball trap devices and consist of two distinctive parts: the ring which fastens just behind the testicles and the tube which encloses the shaft and glans of the penis to keep it contained and prevent erection.

1. The Ring.

Most rings are measured by their diameter, meaning the distance from one side of the ring to another, and these measurements are typically listed on a manufacturer's website in both millimeters and inches. A perfectly sized ring will fit snugly behind your testicles but will continue to allow blood to flow to the penis. It should not pinch or leave your genitals feeling numb or uncomfortable.

Because the penis is round and plump in shape, it is quite difficult to measure the diameter of your or your partner's penis on its own. Therefore, it is recommended that you not only measure the circumference, the full distance around your penis and balls but also perform a simple calculation to determine the diameter from there.

To obtain an accurate measurement of your penis's circumference, it is recommended to first take a hot bath or shower. This will leave your penis flaccid but encourage the active flow of blood so that your final result will account for the slight swelling of the equipment as blood passes through. For best results, take your measurement immediately upon getting out of the shower or bath, before your body has had any time to cool down.

You can measure yourself using several common household objects. A measuring tape is made from yielding cloth which is specifically designed to measure round or irregularly shaped objects. This can be easily wrapped around the penis just behind the testicles. If you do not own a measuring tape, you can instead wrap a length of string, ribbon, or shoelace around your penis, then straighten it out and record its length using a ruler.

Once you've got your circumference measurement, simply divide it by pi (approximately 3.14) to obtain the diameter. Below are a few examples of such calculations using popular ring sizes:

Circumference behind testicles of 6.1 in (157 mm) ÷ 3.14 = ring diameter of 1.96 in (50 mm)

Circumference behind testicles of 5.5 in (141 mm) ÷ 3.14 = ring diameter of 1.77 in (45 mm)

Circumference behind testicles of 4.9 inches (125 mm) ÷ 3.14 = ring diameter of 1.57 inches (40 mm)

If you find your measurement lies between two listed sizes on a manufacturer's website, then use the larger of the two. As your penis shrinks some from longer-term chastity device use, you may need to go to a smaller size.

2. The Tube.

Taking measurements for the long "tube" portion of your device is a significantly simpler process. You can use a straight ruler to measure the length of your penis from the top from the base to the tip. As with the ring measurement, it is recommended to do this right after a hot bath or shower, so that the penis is completely flaccid but there is some active blood flow to the area.

Stand up tall with your back straight. Place the edge of the ruler against the base of your penis and lay it flat on the top of your penis. Then, to obtain the most accurate measurement, press the ruler firmly against your pubic bone. This prevents any belly fat from getting in the way and messing up your measurement. You may wish to ask a partner or trusted friend to help

you with this, as reading the ruler while remaining in a straight, tall posture can be difficult.

When choosing a chastity device, do not look for the tube which most closely matches your shaft in length. Instead, subtract between 1/4 in and 1/2 in (6 and 13 mm) from your measurement. For example:

Flaccid penis length of 4 inches = 3.5 or 3.75-inch tube

Flaccid penis length of 3 inches = 2.5 or 2.75-inch tube

Flaccid penis length of 2 inches = 1.5 or 1.75-inch tube

Flaccid penis length of < 2 inches = 1 or 1.25-inch tube

The ideal tube will fit your penis tightly but not constrict it to the point that it cannot release urine. Ideally, your urethral slit will lie against the opening at the end of the tube. The width of the tube will be narrow and completely prevent you from achieving an erection, no matter how aroused you may become.

Accessories

Just as there are a wide variety of devices, styles, and materials, there is also a huge assortment of accessories that can be purchased to be used with or as part of a chastity device. I will summarize a few here, but you may want to research this topic on your own for ones I have missed.

The most common accessory is a dildo as part of a strap-on or integrated into the device. For males in chastity, they have no use of their erect penis, however, their partner or dominant may want to be penetrated or have another subordinate penetrated. A strap-on dildo works great for this purpose. Designed initially for females to allow them to penetrate a male, they work equally well for males in chastity.

The most common form of this accessory is a strap or belt that is worn around the hips and allows for an attachable dildo for the front that can be worn over or above the chastity device. However, some devices can have a dildo attach directly to them. The Shapeways Cherry Keeper device, which was mentioned in the ball-trap section, has an optional attachment that can be connected using short pins that then allow for the use of a dildo. Care should be taken with integrated devices like this, though, as they are not as secure as a traditional strap-on dildo and may put additional weight on the chastity device.

Another common accessory is the use of a strap or belt that attaches to the base ring and goes around the waist. For males that use metal chastity devices, as I do, the weight of the chastity device can sometimes allow for more movement that can be uncomfortable. This is especially true when walking, running, or exercising. This can be solved by using a strap or belt that goes around the waist and attaches to the base ring on either side. Such straps are sold online by companies such as Amazon, but it is also very easy to make with some no stretch elastic and some snaps as well from the craft store.

Urethral sounds and tubes are another common accessory that can be found with some devices. These sounds and tubes are designed to be inserted into the penis and then locked in place. They can plug the penis or allow for ease in urination in smaller devices, however, in either case, you should exercise extreme caution. Inserting such devices comes with it several dangers including making small cuts in the urethra and associated urinary tract infections. While they are fine for short-term play as long as you thoroughly disinfect them, I would not recommend them for long-term wear.

I mentioned that many males have scrotums that are known as "high and tight". While they will relax and contract to maintain the optimum temperature for the testicles, the average "hang" on any one male will vary. Ball stretchers are often used to stretch the skin and either temporarily or, over time, permanently allow the balls to hang lower. There are many varieties and styles, so I will discuss a few here.

1. Two Piece. First is the two-piece stretcher. It is a basic ring that is usually magnetically held together. You can slowly add or stack rings to force the testicles down in the sack and different diameters are available as well.

2. The Parachute Stretcher: The parachute stretcher looks like it sounds. It is designed to wrap around the scrotum and testicles and has chains that connect to a ring from which weights can be added. These stretchers can often be used in BDSM CBT scenes as well.

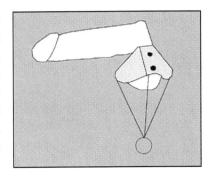

3. The Humbler. This device looks a bit medieval when you first look at it. Often made of wood or hard plastic, it is two flat pieces that are bolted together through the arms. There is a hole or cavity in the center that allows the balls to be placed and held stretched out to the bottom of the scrotum. The arms go under the legs and help to keep tension on the balls and direct them downward.

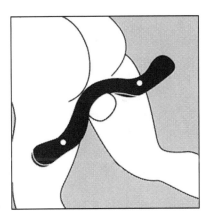

4. All-In-One Stretchers. These devices are typically just a ring that goes against the shaft where the scrotum starts and another that goes against the testicles in the bottom of the sack. They are connected by rods that allow you to increase the space between the rings, thereby forcing the balls lower and lower in the scrotum and stretching it as a result.

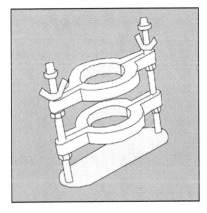

5. Ball Sleeves. Ball sleeves are one-pieces usually made from either metal or silicone that completely encase the testicles and scrotum. Their design can force the testicles lower in the sack, or the weight of the device, if it is metal, can act as a stretching mechanism as well.

These are just a few variations, but there are many more. If you choose to try this, be sure to exercise caution as damage can occur from improper use.

Butt plugs are often another type of accessory as well. These come in a variety of forms, but with the rise of the pup scene, plugs attached to tails are becoming a popular option. I have one of these myself, and although I do not consider myself a pup per se, I have had doms that have enjoyed seeing my tail in before and/or after they get to use my ass in a sexual encounter. The movement of the tail can hit the 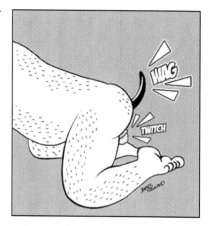 prostate as well and some people have been able to milk themselves from the stimulation of wagging it. I must admit that I have been able to milk myself in this manner in the past.

Finally, there is one aspect of chastity devices that can be truly dangerous. Let's talk about spiked chastity devices. Some devices feature add-ons like spikes, also known as anti-pullout pins, inside the tube itself. Their purpose is exactly as stated, if the male tries to pull out of the device or otherwise break out in any way, the spikes will dig painfully into his penis. If he tries to touch himself and achieve an erection, the same thing will happen.

Anti-pullout pins are dangerous and can cause long-term harm to the penis. Realistically, there is no way to fully prevent every attempt by the penis to become erect. Involuntary nighttime erections will continue to occur (or attempt to occur) even after years of enforced chastity. These are the body's way of making sure blood is circulating properly in the genital area and are extremely healthy and normal. When wearing a spiked device, the anti-pullout pins will dig painfully into the shaft of the penis during these nighttime periods, potentially causing cuts, bruises, and abrasions.

For your safety, I do not recommend the use of a device with spikes and/or anti-pullout pins.

Hygiene

Even if you've found the perfect-sized chastity device, it's still important to keep it clean. An unclean device begins to develop a distinctive odor that's likely to be a turnoff for even the most adventurous of keyholders.

While in chastity, you should shower daily and make cleaning your device a part of your regular hygiene routine. Most devices, especially metal ones, have enough holes, slits, and breathable areas to allow for cleaning the device while it's still locked to your penis. A mobile shower head with a high-pressure setting is one of the best ways to flush out any leftover sweat, urine, or other fluids from your device. If your shower head is of the stationary variety, a squeeze bottle filled with hot water works just as well!

However, it's important to wash off with more than just water. As someone in permanent chastity, I recommend using Q-tips with a small amount of body soap to thoroughly clean the penis. If you regularly experience dry skin, moisturizing lotion can be applied in the same manner, though, as with the soap, make sure to wash the device out thoroughly with hot water after applying.

Make sure to dry the device thoroughly after showering (or bathing, or swimming). Moisture trapped within the device for long periods is the number one cause of unpleasant smells, infections, and skin rashes. A hairdryer on a low or cool setting works excellently for this purpose.

Keyholders should ideally allow their subordinate male out of their device every week for a cleaning session. This can be supervised if you don't trust them to carry this out without sneaking in a little self-pleasure. They can also be restrained or even blindfolded so they are not able to see themselves out of the device.

Once the device is removed, check the penis and testicles for any signs of discoloration, chafing, cuts, bruises, or irritated skin. Small injuries can occur unnoticed during periods of short- and long-term lockup. If anything seems off or wrong, consult a physician.

During the period of release, make sure to clean both the device and the penis thoroughly. I recommend the process I use, which is a 50% vinegar and water solution that you immerse the device in and follow up with a scrub with a toothbrush. You should also use soap and water as well to ensure a good clean. Many males in chastity prefer to trim or shave their genitals to avoid getting pubic hair caught in the device. If you take this route, all trimming and shaving should occur while unlocked.

Shaving the genital area for the first time can cause ingrown hairs, redness, and irritation. If you think long-term chastity might be right for you and have not shaved your genitals before, start before your device arrives to accustom your body to shaving.

Lubrication

Even if you have a good fitting device, it is smart to lubricate. While I know that some disagree on this point, I find that it makes things more comfortable and dramatically cuts down on sores, cuts, and irritation. I lubricate my device every morning after I get out of the shower and apply lubrication to the bottom of the base ring and around the edge of the tube portion of the cage as well. I use a combination of lubricants. One is a silicone lubricant because I just find it works better for me and I use a metal device that will not be harmed by it. However, water-based lubricants are just as good. If you do go the silicone route, you need to be sure to clean well every day to ensure that things stay clean and bacteria-free. Water-based lubricants are easier to clean off than silicone.

Another option you can consider, which is the other lubricant I use, is a product called Aquaphor. This is an ointment that is used to soothe skin irritations and is commonly recommended after getting a tattoo. I rub a small amount of this around the base ring to help keep any irritation at bay around my scrotum area. I have heard of others using simple talcum powder as well. The main thing is you want to monitor and prevent any type of friction here, especially if you are looking into long-term chastity.

Getting Started

What to Expect

Especially at the beginning, it is extremely important to give the body some time and not want too much of it. You should slowly get used to wearing the chastity device. As a male, you should consciously refrain from sexual arousal through porn that would make the feeling worse, but I admit, even I am a glutton for punishment.

For the new chastity user, it's better to be a little slower than to lose your appetite right at the beginning. You should listen to the signs of your body and react accordingly. Each person is different, but if this is something you want to get into for longer and longer periods, I would not take a break that lasts more than three days. This would be a fresh start and is certainly not in your interest.

I also recommend that at first, you orgasm before you lock up. This takes away the frustration element at the very beginning and lets you concentrate on the comfort of the device and what it feels like to have it on. You will also find it is much easier to install without getting constant erections at first.

Start slow, though. Wear it for an hour or two and then take it off and see if you notice any pinching or sore areas. Consider blogging or writing down your thoughts. How does it feel to wear the device? Do you envision yourself wearing it for longer and longer periods? What are some barriers to this thought?

As you get more comfortable with the device, you should work your way up to wearing it all day but take it off before you go to bed. Wait till you can wear it all day for a few days before a 24-hour session. This is because the device will stop nocturnal erections from occurring. Your body will still try to have them, and it will wake you up. You can expect the first night to be woken up at least four to five times and this can be a frustrating experience that breaks the will of a lot of new chastity users.

If you get used to the device and are more comfortable wearing it during the day, then the first night will be frustrating, but will not dissuade you from continuing. Do be aware, though, that it will take time to learn to sleep through the night. I find that sleeping on my side with a pillow between my legs or on my back are the best positions for comfort.

One other thing to note is that as you wear the device for longer periods, you may start to notice more precum production. It has been my experience that I go through cycles where I produce more at times than others. Sometimes this is at night and sometimes it is during the day and sometimes it is both. Nighttime emissions might mean cleaning the sheets the next day, but daytime emissions can be embarrassing if you are at work. You might need to plan to wear a pad or something to soak up the emissions if this happens to you. Female pads or even a sock is a great option for this.

Stages of Chastity

For those that are exploring chastity and orgasm denial, it is important to realize there are many stages that you will encounter in your journey. I ran into a few articles online that I felt best encapsulated some of the feelings and mental experiences. I will discuss a few here.

The first is the "Eight Stages of Chastity". I have seen this presented in many forms from many different authors and websites and sometimes there are fewer or more stages listed but this list pretty well followed my experience as I got started.

> **Stage 1:** The first stage is the discovery stage. It is at this point that you begin to explore and learn about chastity and find that it interests you. You spend time searching on the internet to look at pictures and read stories of those in chastity and you find that you are sexually aroused.

> **Stage 2:** At this stage, you may have started to experiment with edging or resisting the urge to ejaculate for a day, a few days, or even a week. You have not yet determined if you want to purchase a device for yourself, but you find the idea arousing and think of this when you eventually orgasm.

> **Stage 3:** At this stage, you have decided to obtain a device and experiment with chastity. It may only be for a few

minutes to an hour, but the arousal is real and can be part of sexual fantasies.

Stage 4: By stage four, you have decided to move to wear the device for days up to a week. You begin to find that you enjoy having the device on and you begin to think about finding someone to hold your key.

Stage 5: In stage five, you have found a keyholder that helps control your periods in chastity. They may also determine when and if you can orgasm. You have started to embrace chastity as something that fulfills you and you work to move to longer periods in the device.

Stage 6: By stage six, you begin to find that the pleasure of others begins to be on your mind more and more and this makes you feel good. You may be in chastity all the time at this point or making multiple sessions of days to weeks at a time. You begin to find ways to cope with your emotions and hormonal balance. You also long to have the device back on after it is removed.

Stage 7: You are now at a stage where you keep your device on for weeks to months at a time, perhaps even most of the year. While it is still removed for the occasional orgasm, you are happy to return to your device. You begin to get more pleasure from service to your partner or dominant and less so from personal gratification.

Stage 8: By stage eight, you do not wish the device to be removed at all. You may feel like you need to ejaculate, but you understand that it is not the right thing for you. You focus more on the pleasure of others and find that it fulfills you in ways you never thought it could. You may be in permanent chastity or unlocked a few times a year for good behavior, but the device has become a part of your body.

While most people will not experience all eight stages or may find different combinations of them appeal to them, as I have mentioned,

I found that this is how I progressed in my journey into chastity. Another variation on this is the Chastity Cycle.

Locked: You enjoy being locked and the way it increases your level of arousal every day. The constant thoughts of sex excite you and you love the type of sexual energy that just gets more and more with every day you spend locked up. Knowing that you would otherwise let all this arousal go to waste makes you question why you would ever unlock it at all. This feels so much better than any orgasm ever could, and it lasts for as long as you stay locked.

Unlocking: As the days go by, you begin to feel overwhelmed by the sexual energy that you had been enjoying up till now. You try to hold off, but you know that you can't keep going much longer. You still want to, but your desires are so overpowering that they rob you of any self-control you had left. You try to reason with yourself but in the end the arguments for unlocking win.

Unlocked: The freedom you have dreamed of for weeks is finally here. You waste no time and start jerking off as soon as the cage is off. You get that needed orgasm soon, almost too soon to enjoy the process. But it does not matter, as you spend the next day obsessively jerking off and orgasming, releasing that pent-up energy. It feels good to orgasm, but the feeling is fleeting, and you have to go back for more. It is never long enough to satisfy you.

Locking: You have jerked off so much in the last day or so that it has lost its appeal. The climax is great but still pales in comparison to the constant high you get when you are locked. You miss that feeling of constant arousal. You decide to lock up again since the disappointment of being a free male made it clear that you are meant to be locked. Jerking off will not provide that deep level of contentment. You learned something and will endeavor to stay locked for a longer period this time.

In whatever way your journey evolves, for those that pursue it and work towards longer periods, you will note a growing desire to embrace your new role. In many ways, your brain starts to rewire itself as you look to get more pleasure from servicing others and less from the quick self-gratification you received previously from being unlocked.

It is important to point out that often, chastity and orgasm denial is also associated with the subordinate and dominant relationship. I know this was the case for me. I started my chastity journey while single and my goals were more aligned with the sub/dom dynamic. Those into pup play may also find some of the same feelings as I had as well. I have done a lot of research on this topic over the years, and back when I had a daily Tumblr blog, I developed these categories from a variety of sources to explore this dynamic spectrum.

1: Kinky Sensualist – Not into servitude; into spiced-up sensuality; turned on by the thrill of the moment; both the dom and sub have equal gratification.

2: Pseudo Submissive – Will role-play servitude behavior; interested in dom's pleasure but personal gratification as well; self-dictates scene to a large degree.

3: Play Submissive – Gives up control within limits with servitude behavior; interested in dom's pleasure, but personal pleasure as well; does not self-dictate scene

4: Uncommitted Submissive – Gives up control within limits with servitude behavior; dom's pleasure is a priority, but only when the sub is in the mood; does not self-dictate scene and often dom will dictate.

5: Part-time Submissive – Dom is in control; dom's pleasure is the only priority; sub devotes most of its time to commitments (job; but dom decides schedule to a degree; dom dictates the scene.

6: Full-time Submissive – Dom in control; dom's pleasure is the only priority; sub lives with dom and has structured existence.

I will explore this more in Chapter Three of this text where I discuss my journey but know that many people get into chastity for many different reasons and it can be a healthy and safe experience and a rewarding one for both parties. But it is important to think about your goals, what you want and what your limits are. You need to discuss these with your partner or dominant and find ways to meet your needs and theirs, but respect limits as well.

Short-Term Chastity

The headspace for most that get into a short-term chastity lifestyle as part of a relationship is often a circular cycle that repeats: the first time a subordinate male is locked up and then again, after orgasm (whether that is minutes, hours, days, or weeks) the process begins with "Getting to Headspace". However, because this is a model that exists in time, it is a spiral versus a closed circle, because people grow and mature as they go through the process. Thus, each chastity cycle is different and potentially more fulfilling, as males learn from each experience. Conceptually, however, the phases in each cycle are the same or very similar. The following was developed from Devoted Lover (2010) on their blog which discussed this cycle.

1. Getting to Headspace. This is the first phase after a device is placed on a subordinate male and locked. This phase usually does not take long as most subordinate males have been exploring and researching the lifestyle before trying a device on for the first time. Indeed, many subordinate males will come to embrace the "Chastity Nirvana" (headspace) phase more than the process of getting to it and have the experience of knowing how to get there. During Getting to Headspace a subordinate male experiences a variety of feelings including excitement, amazement, a bit of wonder (this is particularly true for subordinate males who have long fantasized about chastity and suddenly are seeing it as a dream come true), and of course, horniness. Negative feelings may also surface, such as crankiness and frustration. These feelings have a yin-yang quality that comes from a very basic conflict that a male is struggling with during this period, that of giving up control. Chastity is a consensual power exchange. Even though a subordinate male may say to his dominant keyholder, "I have given you control," the minute the lock is clicked and the key handed over, I don't think that control is truly and completely given until the subordinate male moves out of the Getting to Headspace phase of the process. The hallmark of this phase is the need for the subordinate male to resolve these conflicting feelings and accept that the dominant keyholder is in control. It is the resolution of this inner conflict that allows the subordinate male to move forward to phase two: Chastity Nirvana.

2. Chastity Nirvana. The peaceful, Zen-like feeling of being locked up accompanied by a desire to want to be locked up. During this phase, a subordinate male can't imagine being any other way and in fact, gets anxious at the thought of not being locked up. The conflict of Getting to Headspace has been resolved and he can fully relax and enjoy the feelings of sexual excitement, tension, arousal, and desire that are present within his body and mind. Finding an appropriate outlet for these feelings is when a subordinate male begins to focus on the object of his desire who is, typically, a partner, dominant, or keyholder. How these feelings are manifested seems to vary. The conventional wisdom suggests that subordinate males become more attentive. This may translate into becoming more helpful around the house, offering to do more chores, and so on. For a subordinate male who hasn't been doing this previously, this might be the most remarkable change a partner or dominant will notice. In fact, for subordinate males who are trying to entice their partners or dominants into a chastity lifestyle, this seems to be the carrot that they dangle. The promise of being a better partner or subordinate, particularly in ways that will be readily apparent, certainly would seem to be an appealing outcome to any dominant.

Beyond household chores, the bigger and more important change comes in the area of sexual relations. Because the subordinate male has resolved his conflict and given up control, he is able now to focus on his partner or dominant. "Their pleasure is my pleasure" is the mantra of Chastity Nirvana. This has been true for me. The challenge sometimes for the dominant keyholder is to fully believe, accept, and embrace this principle. For some partners and dominants, it can take a bit of mental work to realize that the subordinate male is offering up his orgasms, the traditional measure of "pleasure", in exchange for the dominant's complete and total pleasure.

2a. Home Stretch. Chastity Nirvana has two sub-phases. The first is the "Home Stretch". It seems that most subordinate males have some sense of when they are going to be released. Even if they don't know an exact date, dominant keyholders like to drop hints: "around your birthday," "Christmas," "after the first of the year." Some subordinate males do have an exact date and even though that may change, they still anticipate their release. As they get closer to the date, real or anticipated, they move into the Home Stretch.

The Home Stretch seems to be fraught with a tinge of anxiety as well as anticipation. Chastity Nirvana, is, at its essence, a peaceful phase, even though the subordinate male is experiencing a high level of sexual excitement throughout (another paradox of chastity: being highly aroused can be peaceful and Zen-like). In the Home Stretch, the subordinate male begins to anticipate the feeling of being released and the opportunity to orgasm that has been denied for some time. Knowing that "the end is near" heightens the sexual excitement and tension. At the same time, there is anxiety, knowing that if he is released, he will need to begin the entire chastity process again. I think all people tend to resist change and being in the Home Stretch is an anticipation of change and thus stressful. The pleasurable outcome of having an orgasm heightens this internal conflict. Just as Getting to Headspace is a phase of internal conflict, so is the Home Stretch.

2b. Diminishing Returns. While I said that Chastity Nirvana can go on indefinitely, there is a point for most short-term chastity users where the sexual energy and tension of chastity will eventually plateau and then begin to decline. While the fantasy of "permanent orgasm denial" is a powerful one for them, it seems that for the short-term user, subordinate males do need to be released and orgasm to keep the entire cycle of chastity alive. Many couples seem to experiment with prolonged periods of chastity to see just how far they can push the Chastity Nirvana phase and also find where they reach the plateau and decline of Diminishing Returns. Some never seem to get there which is probably why not many people discuss this. However, one person told me that he and his partner have learned that two weeks is their best "length of cycle." He said they did go for a month, once, but after that experience, he discovered that for them, it was better to keep their game short and focused. Realizing that has made it a very positive experience and they are fully committed to their chastity lifestyle.

3. Orgasm. Orgasm is the final phase. In this stage, the pleasure reverts to the subordinate male. "My pleasure is my pleasure" becomes the mantra again. Second, the power goes back to the subordinate male, or at least it becomes more equally shared by the couple. Last, the feelings of anticipation and tension disappear since those factors no longer exist and will not exist again until the subordinate male is in chastity again, either mentally (honor system) or physically by a device.

How much both members of the couple enjoy the feelings of the chastity process will determine how much and how deeply they play the game. For some couples, it is an integral part of their lifestyle. For others, it is a game that is played occasionally. For some subordinate males, it is a game that they play in a somewhat solo fashion if their partner or dominant is unwilling to participate or not fully on board or half-hearted in their interest.

Long-Term Chastity

There are several myths and a large amount of incorrect information regarding the effects of long-term or permanent male chastity. Wearing a chastity device for long periods is safe and healthy if you keep both the device and your genitals clean and remove it in the case of medical emergencies. I should know, I have been in permanent chastity for about four and a half years now. I will address some of the most common of those myths and why they are simply not true.

Myth: Wearing a chastity device long-term will cause erectile dysfunction, difficulty urinating, or other problems with penis function.

> **Truth:** There are no recorded results of any of these effects occurring. Professional urologists consulted on the matter did not find any negative effects of long-term chastity. Many males have been happily locked for years and are still able to maintain erections (when unlocked), achieve orgasm, and urinate normally.

Myth: Wearing a chastity device overnight can cause extreme pain because the penis involuntarily becomes erect multiple times per night.

> **Truth:** A properly fitted chastity device should not cause this problem. However, individuals who normally sleep on their stomachs have reported some minor pain and discomfort due to the device. If you wish to sleep with the device on, it is recommended to sleep on your side or back.
>
> While I do not do this myself, some males in chastity do recommend staying unlocked overnight a few times per month, as nocturnal erections promote regular blood flow to the penis. Nocturnal erections can be thought of as the body stretching or exercising the penis as it does any other muscle. As always, talk to your keyholder to decide if overnight uncaging is right for you.

Myth: Long-term or permanent chastity will make the penis or testicles smaller.

> **Truth:** Every situation is different. Some online blogs of males in chastity have reported a decrease in penis size after years of chastity device use, while some have not. I have lost about 3.8 cm (or 1.5 in) in flaccid length in the four and a half years I have been in permanent chastity.
>
> Extended periods, several months or more, without erection or orgasm, may cause some shrinking of the corpus cavernum (erectile tissue of the penis) due to disuse. However, this is completely reversible once the device is removed and normal blood flow is restored.
>
> If you are concerned about this possibly happening to you, talk to your keyholder about scheduling more frequent orgasms or the aforementioned overnight uncaging periods.

Myth: It is dangerous for a male not to ejaculate for a long time.

> **Truth:** According to medical authorities, there is no adverse effect if a male doesn't ejaculate for months or even years.

According to Pepper Schwartz, Ph.D., "There is some data published by the Journal of American Medical Association that higher emissions were correlated with a lower rate of prostate cancer, but this is over a long period of time-and the increment of health is slight."

Myth: After being locked in a chastity device, a male will become more attentive and interested in his partner.

> **Truth:** A key storyline in many male chastity fantasies is that the male will immediately redirect his sexual energy to pleasing his partner. This, the fantasy says, is the result of the device being locked on his penis. There is no physical difference between being locked in a chastity device and simply abstaining from sex voluntarily. While it is certainly true a caged male will try to find ways to get his keyholder to give him an orgasm, there is no evidence that there is an automatic transference of sexual satisfaction to his keyholder. However, like many myths of this type, if you believe it you can make it true for you.

Myth: There should be some pain associated with wearing a chastity device.

> Truth: This is a big one. A well-designed chastity device should not hurt to wear. Too many males buy inexpensive plastic cages that irritate the skin behind their balls or other areas on their genitals. Some males have no problem wearing them. If you wear or are planning to wear your device for more than a weekend at a time, you should invest in a good-fitting device that you won't even notice most of the time. I wear a Mature Metal Jail Bird 24/7 with no discomfort, but I do lubricate and inspect the device and my genitals regularly for any issues.

Selfcare

The best advice I can give those that are interested in exploring chastity and orgasm denial, whether be by yourself, with a partner, or with a dominant or keyholder, is to do it safely and maintain your selfcare. What I mean by this is you need to seriously consider why you are doing this, set your goals and boundaries, communicate these goals and boundaries with anyone you are exploring this with, and be open and honest with them about your feelings and how your experience is progressing.

Establish boundaries. This is the most critical agreement you will have. Think to yourself and, if applicable, discuss with your partner or dominant how long you will be locked before you get a release. Many males will just say that they don't want a release. You can't possibly know that in the very beginning. Agree to some initial no-sex period.

Discuss what else you must do to earn your orgasm. This is where a dominant can take control and let the subordinate male know that the more he pleases the dominant (not just in the bedroom) the more inclined the dominant will be to unlock him.

Consider establishing a "safe word". This is a word or phrase that the male in chastity can use to indicate he is in real distress, that his cage may be hurting him badly, or that he has an emotional issue, anything urgent. If he uses his safe word, the partner, dominant or keyholder should agree to immediately release him, stop any activities, and discuss the problem.

You should set limits on "chastity chat". In the beginning, it is very easy to get a bit obsessive about this new activity. For both your sanity and that of your partner, dominant or keyholder, agree on how much you can discuss your chastity device. Set fixed times for discussions.

Finally, draw out your expectations. They will almost certainly be more than you will want, at least at first. This is the time to agree very explicitly on what will happen in the near future. Repeat this frequently as you get more experience.

Take care of yourself. Your penis is under another's control or your self-control. Another person might have the key and you cannot access it without another person's agreement. Pretty much every chastity device will cause some physical issues, particularly in the beginning. It's a good idea to remove the cage every few days and inspect yourself. Look for sores and redness. If you see any, consider leaving yourself unlocked to give yourself a chance to heal. You may need to order a different device or send the one you have back for adjustment. This is a normal part of the process. Once things fit right, you will need to inspect less often, and you won't need to be uncaged unless you want to be (and the dominant allows). Being unlocked does not mean you get an orgasm. If the cage is off because you need a new one or you need to heal, you need to exercise self-control and not touch yourself. Chastity is less about the actual device and more about the mindset.

Don't push yourself or let yourself be pushed further than you want to go. If your partner, for instance, is not used to being the "boss", that will not change simply because you are in a chastity device. The worst thing is to allow a subordinate to "top from the bottom". This means that while the dominant appears to be in control, the subordinate in chastity is manipulating the dominant into doing what he wants. You need to discuss your roles with your partner, dominant or keyholder, and make sure everyone is comfortable with the roles and most importantly, you need to understand that you are giving up a little control. Male chastity is about the desire to surrender control. The dominant, thus, needs to enforce the boundaries you set.

Don't quit too soon. Male chastity may not be easy for you or your partner/dominant, especially in the beginning. If you become difficult or cranky, or if you start to annoy your partner or dominant with endless chastity talk, the temptation on their part is just to end it or quit participating. Try to not let this end your experiment prematurely. Even if it is something you truly are interested in and they are supportive, it is a big adjustment. You might agree to a trial period and then discuss how things went and how to proceed.

Talk, Talk, Talk. This leads me to the final self-care suggestion: talk about it! Males are famous for not wanting to discuss their feelings. We males will try to turn any "feeling" conversation into something more "objective". You need to force yourself to be open and honest about what you want, how you want to proceed, what it means to you, how your partner or dominant feels, and discuss any points of friction. Even if you are doing this on your own, blog about it, seek out advice from others that have been in chastity, and discuss your questions and feelings. In the long run, it will help you more than you know.

Psychology of Chastity

When a male has an orgasm, his brain releases a chemical called dopamine. Dopamine makes you happy, physically, and emotionally. It's that high you get when you complete a task or reach a goal or eat your favorite meal and suddenly you feel like you could take on the world.

The male orgasm is one of, if not the, most potent shots of dopamine your brain can get. After orgasm, the brain follows up with a second chemical, known as prolactin. Prolactin relaxes you; it causes the sluggish "afterglow" feeling that follows a really good orgasm.

In males, prolactin forces dopamine to leave your system quickly. This is the reason that the average male orgasm tends to be short (lasting only 5-10 seconds) and the tired post-coital feeling comes on so quickly. But what does a male orgasm look like after a month of being snugly denied within a chastity device?

Studies show when a male orgasms after a significant period of denial (usually several days to several weeks), his brain releases more dopamine and less prolactin, allowing for a longer, more intense orgasm. Additionally, the dopamine stays in his system longer, for up to several days after orgasm, allowing him to continue feeling happy and energized. In short, there is a valid scientific reason why enforced male chastity produces longer and better orgasms with pleasurable, beneficial aftereffects.

But what about a male in permanent chastity that gives up orgasms? This is a question I get a lot since this is what I have done. I can tell you that the first few months can be very difficult as you begin to embrace and understand you may never be getting out of your device and you may never achieve orgasm again. However, the brain can overcome this.

For the permanently chaste male, the loss of orgasms leads the brain to seek out new ways to achieve pleasure. Over time, pleasing others and bringing your partner or dominant to orgasm can cause your brain

44

to release dopamine as well. Indeed, you can, over time, learn to feel just as much pleasure from the pleasure of others and getting them to orgasm. Once you achieve this state, you don't need a traditional orgasm anymore.

Not everyone can achieve this state, and if you cannot and you need to set a goal to have at least one orgasm or several a year to keep yourself in a good mindset, do not be ashamed of this. The point is to not only please your dominant but also find pleasure in chastity yourself.

Keyholders

When you first start in chastity, you are more than likely going to be controlling your key to your device. In the beginning, this is not an issue. The point is to get comfortable with the device and to ensure it is a good fit. However, if you are going to truly embrace the experience, you need to remove the access to your key for some time.

For those that are single, like me, I was at a loss as to where to turn or what to do. Things have changed a lot in the half-decade I have been exploring chastity and newcomers have a lot more options when it comes to solo locks and self-control.

Finding a Keyholder

If you are single and looking for someone to hold your keys, be careful. There are a lot of males out there that will offer to hold your key, have you mail it to them, or have you rivet or seal a cage shut. You do not want to be in a situation where you try this and then they ghost you and you are left with no escape. Thankfully, there are some better options.

For singles, there are apps you can get for your phone. One I highly recommend is called Chastikey. For this to work, you must purchase a combination lockbox that has at least four number dials on it (the more the better). The app gives you a code to set your box to, you put the keys in, and then it flashes numbers on the screen at you for a set period to help you forget the code. Then, after a certain amount of time that you or others set, you are given the code. You can also play games to get the code as well. This works well for those that are single or have friends remotely that want to become a keyholder.

Similarly, purchasing a Bluetooth or internet-capable lockbox is also an option for those that are single or have friends online that are willing to "hold" your key for you and let you out at an appointed time. There are even chastity cages that have built-in Bluetooth capabilities so the lock can even be controlled online.

If you are in a relationship or have a local dominant or friend that is willing to be an in-person keyholder, this of course is preferable and even more secure. Be sure to set boundaries and how long you plan to stay locked and ensure that whomever you trust your keys with will be willing to hand them back over not only when the time is up, but if an emergency arises.

I should mention at this point that regardless of what method you choose, you need an emergency contingency. For instance, I have two keys to my device. When I had an in-person keyholder, I used to let him hold one key and I kept the other in a sealed container with a plastic numbered lock. If I broke the lock to get at the key, he would know, but in an emergency, I could have access to unlock. This has happened to me before when I had to go to the hospital for emergency surgery, so you never know when you might need access.

If you don't know anyone locally but want someone to help you as a keyholder virtually, then websites such as Recon or Fetlife may be an option. I should caution you though that you should be very careful when trusting anyone online with your key or access to your key. There are a lot of people out there that enjoy the pain and suffering of others, especially in the BDSM arena and I don't mean in a good way. I have seen too often people get taken in and send their keys off or agree to a Chastikey session and things did not work out well. This is not only stressful and can ruin the experience for you, but it can be dangerous as well.

Setting Boundaries

I have mentioned before the importance of setting goals, boundaries, and expectations when you get into chastity, especially for longer terms. Everyone has hard limits they do not want to cross. For me, for instance, I set hard rules with my keyholders and dominants that I do not like extreme pain, the sight of blood, biting, or spanking. I also have several soft rules as well. Whatever your boundaries might be, you need to think about them.

My advice is that you write down why you are getting into chastity, what you expect to get out of it, what you expect your keyholder to provide for you, what you expect to provide your keyholder, and any hard and soft limits you have. They can then read over this and start a discussion with you before you start any formalized keyholding session.

You may even formalize things in a form of a contract that both parties sign and both have copies of. You can find numerous examples of such agreements online, but the main theme is transparency, openness, and understanding about not only what you want, but what your keyholder wants and what limits are being set as well for a safe and healthy experience for both of you.

Developing a Relationship

I have many friends that are in relationships or dating someone that does not know anything about their desire to explore chastity. They often ask me what my advice is, and I can honestly say the most common thing I tell them is to talk to their partner. You need their buy-in. If they are not interested, discuss how this is something that you want to try and if there is anything they are interested in that you can try with them in exchange. However, you should be prepared if your partner says no.

This can be a sticking point in a relationship. If you have an equal one where you switch between top and bottom, you are removing one side of the equation that your partner might enjoy. It is important to discuss how this does not have to be the case and how you can still pleasure them, perhaps even more, if you are in chastity.

If you are dominant and interested in your partner getting into chastity play and they are hesitant, a conversation is even more important. Don't push! The quickest way to destroy a relationship is to not take into account the feelings or desires of your significant other. You might also reach out to others that are more experienced in chastity and get their opinions, especially if they are friends in real life.

Chastity can also lead to relationships between the locked male and the keyholder and these relationships can be complicated. My first long-term keyholder was not interested in a formal relationship, but we agreed to one day a week that I would visit and explore things that interested me and pleased him. I have also had a keyholder in another country that I would do daily photo check-ins and record videos with. Over time we expressed an interest in perhaps more, but things did not work out in that case. However, I know of plenty of people that have developed strong connections with their keyholders to the point they moved in with them and started a more formal relationship.

CHAPTER THREE

Long-Term Chastity – A Journey into Permanent Chastity

The Author's Journey

Now that we have discussed some of the physical and medical implications of chastity and orgasm denial, I want to turn to the questions that I get often surrounding permanent chastity. I have been in permanent chastity with orgasm denial since February 2016. In that time, I have changed a lot physically and mentally and there are several lessons I have learned along the way. If there is one thing that I am constantly asked is how do you deal psychologically with long-term or permanent chastity and/or orgasm denial and how do you keep yourself sane, healthy, and motivated. I will discuss my journey and try to address these topics along the way.

Starting at the Beginning

Like many males, I started my journey into the world of chastity and orgasm denial by looking at images, reading posts, and seeing articles on the internet. At the time, this was the social application Tumblr, which has since banned such materials on its platform. I considered myself switch in the bedroom and topped as much as I bottomed, but I had always been interested in exploring the subordinate side of my personality. The person I had been dating was not into kinks at all, so it was not until we broke up that I decided to explore the world of chastity and get my first device.

It was sometime in January of 2015 that I purchased my first chastity device. I came home from work to find a package sitting in my box at the apartment complex. I immediately rushed inside and opened it. It was a cheap metal ball-trap cage that I purchased online for something like twenty US dollars. I was so turned on by the thought of actually trying on a device for the first time that I ended up having to get ice to put on my genitals to get things to calm down so I could get the ring on.

The one thing I immediately noticed was that the base ring was too small. This was going to be a common issue for me in the years ahead. Unlike the majority of the world, it seems, I need a ring size that is larger than the standard sizes provided by just about every manufacturer out there. But this was just for an experiment, so I pushed through some of the pain and got things on, and clicked the lock closed.

It was a head rush. I must tell you that looking at pictures and reading other people's blogs and posts are one thing, but putting on a device is a completely different experience. I was only able to keep it on for about thirty minutes before I had to remove it and jack off, but I was hooked from the start. I was nervous about the ring size though, so I reached out to a local friend that I had for advice. He suggested I try the CB-6000 since it came with a few different ring sizes and spacers to experiment with. He also lent me a spare CB-Curve cage he had without the ring.

So, I took the plunge and put down the money for the CB-6000 ball-trap cage. While waiting for it to arrive, I continued to experiment with the metal cage I had. Working my way up to an hour and then a few hours and then half a day before the pain got too much from the smaller ring. I learned that if I lubricated the ring, I could manage it for longer periods, and I remember well the first day I went all day with it on at work. I was lubricating about every two hours and I made a mess in my pants of precum, but it was a rush.

When my new CB-6000 came in the mail, I was interested to see how the plastic device would work. It took a long time to force my shaft into the cage portion, though. At that time, I was pretty girthy and long in the non-erect state and getting things to fit without getting aroused could take up to 15 minutes. I found again that the largest ring they had was still too small for me, but with lubrication, I could make it work.

Over the next month, I worked up to longer and longer periods in the device. I made it through my first night, but it was tough, to say the least. I must have woken up at least five to six times that night every time my body tried to have a nocturnal erection. I was so exhausted the next morning that I questioned moving forward, but I persisted and the next night I tried again, and it was not as bad. By the end of the month, I had worked myself up to two days in the device before the urge to unlock and orgasm became too great to overcome.

My Keyholder

The next logical step was to move from self-locks and having access to the key to having someone hold the key for me. I was lucky in that my friend was willing to help me with this. So, on Friday, March 6, 2015, I headed over to his place after work to drop off the key and drive home with my CB-6000 locked on. I was leaking precum the entire way home and nervous as to how this would go. We agreed to a weekend session whereby I would wear the cage till Sunday night and then come over to get released.

For anyone that has ever gone through the first session with a keyholder, not having access to your key hits you quickly. When I got home, I was precumming like crazy and the more I thought about the cage, the more I would get attempted erections. I used a washcloth with ice to calm things down and watched TV and tried to find things to distract me. That night I woke up a few times, but I had done night sessions before, so I managed. The next day, though I was horny as hell and knew I was not getting out that day and had no choice in the matter. It was a unique experience and challenges your thought process behind chastity. For me, I realized that tomorrow was my release day and I could do this and so I persevered.

Sunday morning, I woke up to find my sheets covered in precum. I was leaking bad and the thought I was getting out that evening was making me pop attempted erections all day. I could barely make it till that evening when I drove over, and he used the key to unlock me. I jacked off immediately after and orgasmed within sixty seconds. It was an intense experience as well.

My friend and I talked, and we discussed what I was thinking, how the past few days went, and what I wanted to do in the future. He was experienced in this and was a dominant for a few people and held the keys to one other guy. He asked if I would be interested in letting him hold my key again and perhaps serving him in a few ways, but if I agreed, there would be conditions attached. He brought out some paper and we wrote down some rules. I let him know what things were off the table for me and he discussed things he likes subs to do for him. We agreed on an emergency option for me to get access to a key and communication protocols and such and then he said that he expected me to be locked for thirteen days for the next session. The thought of two weeks made me pause. Honestly, he was pushing me a bit and probably moving too fast, but it was more a test to see what I would say.

He waited as I sat there and thought. Honestly, the excitement got to me and I agreed. He told me to sign on the line and he noted that if I made it, he would promise to give me the fuck of my life and let me cum as much as I wanted after. He handed me a lockbox and told me that I could jack off my "nub", as he called it, as much as I wanted tonight but tomorrow morning, I would put the device back on, put the keys in the box and close it. I could text him at any time if I needed the code to get out.

That evening I started thinking about it a lot. Was I going to go through with this? Could I make it two weeks? Was I crazy? The last part was probably true. I was moving a bit too fast and I should have given myself some time to work up to that length of time, but I was new and green to this and just dove in. So, Monday morning rolled around, and I had one last wank and then locked the cage on and locked the keys away.

Wednesday was the day I started getting a case of blue balls really bad. As I mentioned in chapter one, blue balls are often caused by repeated erections or attempted erections in my case, and no release or orgasm. The feeling is uncomfortable, and I wrote in my Tumblr blog that day that, "I am reminded by the dull ache in my balls and the bulge made by my chastity cage that my keyholder owns my nub." It was a truly humbling experience and I was just getting started. I still had a week and a half to go.

By Friday, I was having issues with the cage. I was constantly using lubricant, sometimes every hour or two, but the ring was too small and uncomfortable. I did not have any sores or bleeding, but it was not a fun experience to be sure. I was precumming so much as well. It seemed like it was getting worse every day. It had got to a point that I was putting a sock in my pants to catch it all at work, which is something I started doing later and continue to do to this day on heavy flow days. I posted on my Tumblr blog, "Haven't cum in a week... would love a cock up my ass to distract me.... like BAD!" I meant it as well.

My keyholder texted me that he read my post and we discussed how things were going. I talked through some things with him and he helped me as I articulated my frustrations, but my interest in continuing. He told me that he would be willing to come over the next day and help. So, on Saturday, he stopped by my apartment and said that while he had intended to wait till my lockup period had elapsed to fuck me he would be willing to reward me now since I made it a week. I did not even have to think. I dropped my pants and bent over the couch and begged for it.

One thing you will learn when you go for longer sessions in a chastity device is that any stimulation is a reward. He was not a small fellow and he mounted me right there in my living room and I was glad I kept some lube on the table. The feeling of him hitting my prostate was wonderful and he milked me as he worked me over for several minutes. When he finally came, I was still horny as hell and sore but felt a lot better.

The next week proceeded like the first. Having my prostate milked helped with the blue balls feeling though and gave me new energy to move forward. By Wednesday I had asked and my keyholder had agreed to allow me to ride a dildo that evening to milk myself again. I did not orgasm but having my prostate drained made a ton of difference once again. I sent him the video as well and apparently, he jacked off to it that night.

When Saturday, March 21 rolled around, my agreed-to unlock date, I was elated. I was also proud of myself that I had made it that far and had the self-control to continue. When I headed over to his house that afternoon, I stayed hard in the cage the whole time. Once he fucked the living hell out of me again, he removed the cage and let me jack off and I shot the hugest load I think I have ever shot. The feeling was intense, and I nearly collapsed. I jacked off thirty minutes later as well.

Just like at the end of the last session, we had a long talk. We discussed my feelings and, if I wanted to continue, what I wanted to learn and explore. I told him I did want to continue, but I asked for a shorter session next time as the pain from the poorly fitting ring was getting to me and I had a wedding to attend the following weekend. We agreed to a five-day session but with one day for me to relax and jack off as much as I wanted.

Monday, I was back in the cage and made it the week with no issues and then was released for my trip that weekend. When I returned, it was back in the cage, but this time I tried the CB Curve cage that was given to me some time ago. It was larger than the CB-6000 tube and was a lot easier to get into, but it was so large that the bulge in my pants was enormous. I wore loose clothes all that week and decided that I would not use the cage in the future. Plus, the extra length meant I could get a bit more erection in the tube which meant a bit more pain and more time for the blood to drain back out as well.

At the end of that session, I returned to my keyholder's house (I had started calling him Sir by this point) and got to suck a load out of him and get one from him bent over in his playroom as well. It was a hot session and afterward, I had another mind-blowing orgasm when unlocked.

We agreed that I would move back to the CB-6000 again for another session. We had not discussed the length of time this go around, and I had assumed it would be a week. When I returned the following week, I drained him good, but he told me that I would be going another week and did not release me. The release would come the following week and from that point, I started sessions that would last varying amounts of time.

In addition to my chastity, my Sir allowed me to explore some other aspects of the dom/sub relationship that I was interested in. I have always liked pleasing others and getting him to climax was great, but I wanted to do more. Over time, I started to do little things for him like making drinks and cleaning things up when I visited. We would explore different aspects of bondage and discipline in his play space and I got a feel for what it was like to be a sub and service a dominant and to start to put their needs first.

Going for Longer Sessions

The sessions continued until the first of May when he turned the key, put it in the lockbox, and then told me that he felt I was getting too used to defined lengths and set days for release so he was not going to tell me how long this session would last. After two weeks, he still had not given me an answer and by the third week, I was begging him. He agreed to tell me a date and set it at thirty days from the time the lock was put on. He told me that if I could make it that long, then we could re-evaluate how things were going and consider some long-term goals for me. It was going to be my longest session yet, but I was committed to moving forward.

On June 3, this is what I wrote in my blog:

> "My keyholder fucked the hell out of me and made a mess of my ass, but I got my release! He sat me down after I was released and orgasmed and we discussed what I wanted moving forward. He had suggestions for other key holders if I wanted them, but if I wanted to continue with him, I needed to start to think more about longer and longer sessions and he expected more of a subordinate relationship for me where

I am more here to service him and other doms. He agreed to give me some time to think about this and we will meet again."

While I was on my break with my Sir, I let another friend hold my key for me as I still wanted to continue in chastity, but the whole time was a reflection point for me to consider my future and what I wanted out of chastity as well.

That session also started with a new chastity cage as well. I had purchased a Bon4 device online. I had researched this device and it came with a much larger ring than standard devices and it made all the difference in the world. I was able to step down to lubricating only a few times a day and the comfort level was at a point that there were times when I forgot that the device was even on me.

After the American July 4 holiday, I met back up with Sir, and I agreed that I wanted to continue to train with him and work to be in chastity for longer periods. By this time, I was hooked. My desire for chastity was high and I enjoyed getting trained to be a good sub as well. Sir provided a safe place to experiment, learn and discuss things as well which made it a perfect place for me to grow. We set up a specific day of the week I would visit him and certain protocols I would follow as well.

The first of these protocols is that on my designated day, I needed to arrive on time. He gave me a key to his side door in his house and a place to undress when I arrived and store my clothes and personal items. I was to be completely naked, except for my chastity device, always in his house unless otherwise instructed. The next protocol involved how I greeted him. I was to kneel next to the front door and silently wait for him to get home from work on the days he was in the office. If he was home, I was to prepare a drink for him and bring it to him in the living room, the latter I was to do after he arrived home from work as well. I addressed him as Sir and we also set down firm limits on what I did not want to experience and a safe word as well.

The session I was in lasted another month and in the end, I was ready to orgasm again. However, he put a twist on my release at this point. Here is what I wrote in my blog later that day:

56

"Sir told me that I did such a good job servicing him that he told me he would unlock me and let me cum. However, the condition was that it had to be his way. He had brought some numbing lube with him and after he unlocked me, he coated my nub and made me sit and look at it for five minutes. By then, I was pretty numb. He then granted me five minutes to jack-off and cum if I could. I furiously took to it and was able to finally bust a nut just before time ended. However, it was a tough thing to do and I didn't get much enjoyment out of it. Still, I was grateful for the release. Sir then cleaned my nub off with a washcloth and then re-locked me again. He thinks it is time to take it up a notch now and go for forty-five days. If I make it and do a good job servicing him in the meantime, then I will get another chance to cum, but this time I will only have four minutes to try with the numbing cream. I've never been locked up more than about thirty days so, this will be a bit of a challenge, I have to admit, I am also a bit worried at the thought of whether I will get to cum in the short period I will have next time."

So, the next session started with a timer set at forty-five days. I still had my weekly visits with Sir, and he would milk me at least every second session if not weekly, depending on how well behaved I was. In doing so, I was able to stay focused and keep my prostate healthy and stay orgasm-free for my lock-up period as well. I also was tasked with answering questions that people sent me to my blog. Many of these questions have been addressed in earlier chapters of this text, but one I got was a pretty common one which I will post here with the answer I provided.

"I ran across your blog via a re-blog, I have never done chastity, but just wondered if you have issues with erections, especially at night? I can imagine it must be painful in that device. Also, what is it like not to cum for so long? I cannot imagine going so long without."

That is usually the first question people ask me if they find out I am in chastity. My nub still tries to get erect from time to time, that is a natural process. However, the cage limits the extent of the erection and forces some of it internally. It is uncomfortable at first. You must find a device that works for you and that you can tolerate. But you get used to it after a while. You must be careful though. I keep my ball sack well lubricated with lotion to reduce the chance of chafing, which I have had issues with in the past when I was first starting out. As far as erections at night, well at first, I woke up constantly at night due to the strain of an attempted nocturnal erection, but I don't notice them anymore. I don't know if that means I don't have them or if I am just used to the feeling and sleep through it. I do still wake up from time to time if I have had a very erotic dream. As far as what it is like, well it can be frustrating. You get this very full sensation in your balls; some would call blue balls, I guess. My Sir is good to me as he usually straps me down and milks me every few weeks to release the pressure. So, that feeling kind of goes away but you still don't get the release you get with an orgasm. But it is not for everyone. I just enjoy serving Sir. When he gets off thanks to my help, that does wonders for me.

By the end of the forty-five-day session, I was ready to pop, but as I mentioned my release came with a big caveat, I had to follow his rules in my attempt to orgasm. I'll post what he wrote in his blog later that evening to summarize the experience that I had:

> I instructed the boy to arrive promptly at my house at 6:30 pm, enter through the side door, strip, and fold his clothes neatly by the door and then wait for me by my front door till I arrived. I eventually showed up around 7 pm to find him head bowed and on his knees waiting patiently for me. He has been good and made it forty-five days in chastity with no slip-ups, so as promised I told him I would give him the chance to orgasm.
>
> I told him to stand and I unlocked his chastity device and inspected his nub to make sure there were no issues. I then had him wash it in the sink and I rubbed some lotion on him to make sure he was not chaffed. I then had him follow me to the back room where I had previously set out the equipment he would be using for his attempt.

The boy was presented with two condoms, some numbing cream, and a Fleshlight masturbation device to put his small nub into to attempt to cum.

I first had the boy coat his nub in a generous amount of the numbing cream. I wanted to make sure it was soaked in good, so I had him do this several times to provide a thick coat.

After cleaning his hands with a washcloth, I instructed him to place the first condom on and then the second. I inspected this to make sure that they were securely in place.

I then instructed the boy to put his hands behind his back and I massaged his nub to make sure he could get hard and the cream was soaking in good. I asked the boy if he could feel anything and he replied that he was numb. I then started the timer on my phone and told him he had five minutes to insert his nub in the Fleshlight masturbation device and see if he could orgasm.

Forty-five days ago, he was able to orgasm within five minutes with just the numbing cream and I had intended to reduce the time this session. I think that boys should be trained to orgasm quickly since cumming is just a reward from me, not something to take their time with. I also like the numbing cream as it takes some of the pleasure away because again, this is just a reward, not something to enjoy. However, I felt that keeping him at a limit of five minutes was fair given he had to work under the additional constraints of condoms this time. Plus, it was going to be fun to watch.

The boy inserted his nub into the Fleshlight masturbation device and did his best, furiously pounding it while I timed. It was quite amusing I must say, and I even took a video in addition to the pictures for my viewing pleasure later. He gave it his all and was groaning and putting his hips into it, but It was quite clear, however, that the boy was just not up to the task, though. Near the end, his nub was softening, and he was having trouble getting it in the device. He slipped out twice. Still, I let him continue to try.

At five minutes, I called time, however, and told him to pull out. Poor thing just didn't want to orgasm badly enough. Maybe forty-five days just wasn't enough time. I must admit, I've had boys that stayed in chastity for much longer periods in the past.

I had him pull the condoms off and clean up the large amounts of numbing cream still left unabsorbed. He was upset with his performance at this point, but I promised him that we would try again in fifteen days and he would have a chance to redeem himself and attempt to show that he can orgasm as a real man can. I then locked him up again.

However, just to make sure that he didn't feel the night was wasted, I had him bend over the bed and I rode him for a good long while till he got a load out of me. Then, I groped his balls a bit and smacked his full ass and sent him home.

Forty-five days turned into sixty days and I was going for a full two months this time in the device. Things continued as before and then I got another try with similar protocols at the end of the additional two weeks that were added. Here is the blog post I made that evening after:

I showed up at Sir's place tonight, stripped, and waited for him on my knees as I usually do. He came home and inspected me and told me he wished me luck in my attempt to orgasm. He had me go to the back room and kneel in front of the bed.

As I waited, he got his phone and made me watch the video of my attempt from two weeks ago. Watching my attempt last time got in my head. He said he had enjoyed watching the video over the past couple of weeks and was hoping for a better performance tonight. So, he had me stand and he unlocked my nub and inspected it. He then presented me with the same equipment from a couple of weeks ago.

He told me that he was only going to make me wear one condom this time since he felt like I deserved that small reward for going so long successfully. So, my first job was to use the numbing cream on my nub. He made me use it a lot as he likes to have a good coat in. I hate the stuff because it makes my nub feel numb as hell. I can't feel anything and it's real torture. Of course, that's the point, though.

Once I had a good coat that he approved of, I put on the condom and he inspected me one more time and massaged my nub to get it hard and make sure everything was ready.

I had a pretty raging erection, well good for me, and I was ready to try this time. My balls were so full. I knew I could do it. So, he started the timer and gave me five minutes to insert my nub in the flashlight masturbation device and try to get off.

I did have a bit more feeling this time, even though my nub was mostly numb. I think the fact I only had one condom instead of two this time made that difference. Let me tell you I fucked the ever-loving shit out of that toy. Sir even stepped in and held it for me as I worked it over. I even knocked a few things off the headboard because I was pounding the bed so much. Sir was kind of impressed at my attempt, though he was laughing a bit.

It took a while, but I finally felt that feeling starting to build in my groin and realized I was nearly there. I started grunting and started pounding trying to release, but just then Sir called time and put his hand on my nub and the toy to stop me. I must admit I cursed, and I was devastated because I knew if I just had another thirty seconds, hell fifteen seconds, I could have orgasmed. That feeling that you are so close but denied is unnerving. However, rules are rules and Sir had me pull out.

I told him I was close; like literally, I thought I would orgasm if I touched my nub. So, he had me wait a few minutes to let things calm down. That was even worse. I could feel that blue balls feeling, that feeling that you just want to cum right then and all you need is a few strokes, but I wasn't allowed to try. Finally, after a few minutes, Sir had me remove the condom and clean up a bit. He then re-locked me in my cage.

Sir told me that he would give me another attempt in fifteen days. In my head, I knew that I was so close this time and if I worked a little harder, I could orgasm the next time. That numbing cream was just killer. It makes it tough to get off.

He told me someone had to orgasm and since it wasn't going to be me, it was going to be him, so he directed me over to a fuck bench he has and he forced me down and pounded me for a good while till I got his load. He then shoved a plug in my ass and told me to wear it home and not to take it out till he directed me to. He also told me to think about my attempt and how I can perform better next time.

Another two weeks were added, and I was going for 75 days total at that point. Still, the regular milkings helped my prostate and the blue balls feeling, and to be honest, I started to enjoy being in my device. It is a weird feeling to explain, but over time, I started to embrace chastity as a way of life and started to think about the cage as an extension of my body. I don't know if others feel this way when they work their way up to longer sessions, but for me, it was a mental change that helped me cope.

By the end of the seventy-five days, I was ready to orgasm. Sir set things up like before, but this time I was able to just break through the wall and orgasm with a few seconds left on the clock. I came so hard that I nearly collapsed and filled the condom up a whole lot more than I have ever done before. Sir also gave me a few days reprieve out of the device as a reward and although I was allowed to orgasm as much as I wanted, I only did it once more during that break. I was longing to get back into my cage again.

My next session was a sixty-day period, which was less than the seventy-five that I had completed, so I figured that it was doable. As I have said, by this time, the cage was a part of me, and I was really in the groove. I had learned how to push through the horny days and find ways to be distracted and set myself my goal to make it those sixty days and do it with as few complaints as possible.

As I mentioned, I wanted to start to explore some more sub/dom dynamics with Sir including BDSM and CBT techniques. I would blog about these as they happened each week, but here is an example of one session from my Sir's blog at the time so the reader can get a feel for what I am talking about.

> The boy just left here a bit ago. I usually have him over on Tuesdays to service me and so I can inspect his locked nub for hygiene and health. He is about two weeks into a two-month session, though I am contemplating changing the duration. We will see.
>
> I try to push his boundaries, within agreed limits, a bit to train him as a sub when he is here. Today we worked on sensory deprivation and light CBT. I tied him up to a Saint Andrew's cross in the playroom and blindfolded him. I then put a ball gag in his mouth. I proceeded to pull and play with his locked nub. I put a parachute ball stretcher on him and hung some weights to it to work his balls down. I am working on stretching his balls when I can, so they swing freely below the cage. He is one of those boys with "high and tight" balls. I then placed some nipple clamps on him and proceeded to slightly hit his balls a bit with the end of a crop. Was fun watching him bounce and groan. He even was beginning to precum a bit, which the boy tends to do a lot I have noticed. I stuck a condom on the end of this cage to collect it all.
>
> After I had had my fun with him, I took off the clamps and the ball weights and let him down but left the blindfold and gag on. I then moved him over and bent him over the fuck bench and rode him good for about fifteen minutes to empty my balls. After slapping his ass, a bit to reward him for a good job, I reached down and removed the condom from the front of his cage, which at this point was full of precum. I removed his gag and blindfold and handed him the condom and told him to swallow and lick the condom clean of its contents. I don't want him wasting any of his vital fluids. After that, I had him dress and leave. It was another good session.

So, you can see some of the dynamics that we had and some of the things we would explore when I visited him on my day of the week. Just after thirty days had elapsed, he had me come over for my scheduled visit and we had a talk about my session and how he would like to have it modified. As I blogged about here:

> Sir messaged me to say he was horny, and he wanted me to stop by. I got down on my hands and knees after a time and acted as a footrest while he watched college football and got his drinks and food. At one point, he dropped a load in my ass and plugged me with a butt plug, and then returned to watch the halftime report.

> While there, we talked. Another local boy had expressed interest in subbing for him and he informed me that he will likely be taking him on this week. That means that he will need to spend some time with the new sub to get him up to speed on Sir's rules and expectations. However, the new guy is also experienced and will be starting at ninety days of chastity under Sir. Meaning he would be starting at a longer period than I am under now.

> Sir informed me that he wanted to modify my current time to add thirty days to make my current session ninety days as well. He also informed me he feels I need to embrace being a sub and to stop focusing on my release date. He noted in our conversations that I even mentioned that I wanted to push myself and I wanted to learn more. To that end, he wanted to challenge me to make the next session one hundred eighty days after that. At that point, he wants me to think about my role and wants me to consider permanent chastity as a requirement of continuing to be trained under him. I was a bit shocked at first and it is a big decision. He understood this and is giving me some time to think about it.

> Basically, under these rules, this means that I would be let out once in late January and not again till July. After that point, I would never have an orgasm again, at least under his control. Thus, I had to think about it. Sir was kind enough to let me know though that if this was too much, I could leave his

service with no hard feelings. He is just trying to push me to be a better sub, as I had expressed to him that I had wanted to do, and I do appreciate his efforts.

For the time being, I have decided to accept his request and modify my current session to ninety days. That will exceed my current record time of seventy-five days, which was the last session. I do appreciate what he has done for me in expanding my horizons and treating me well, and I hope that things can continue.

Sixty days became ninety days and I started to consider what it would be like to embrace permanent chastity and grow beyond the confines of the experiences I had gone through so far. I will admit, it was a scary time and I journaled about it, had conversations with him about it often, and tried to think about what would not only make me happy but would also further my growth and goals.

At the end of the next month, he had a couple of subs over including me to what amounted to an orgy. We were the party favors and made sure all the guests were pleasured and had a great time, and to be honest, it was a blast for me as well. I was living the dream of a sub in chastity and it crystallized in my mind that the journey I was on worked for me and I could push myself to the next step.

The Permanent Decision

I eventually had a realization that I wanted to make the leap to permanent chastity sooner than later. Thus, on January 14, 2016, I called Sir and we set aside time to meet over coffee. I told him that while it scared me at first, I wanted to push myself and felt that permanent chastity was for me. We discussed a one hundred eighty-day session after the current session ended, but I wanted to forgo that and start permanent after the current session instead. I did ask for the chance to orgasm one last time, though, just to have something to not only look forward to but remember in hindsight as well. Sir was pleased I had made the decision but wanted to modify the orgasm request. He wanted to have it done his way, with the numbing cream and if I could not do it the first time, I would be given some extra time and then a second chance, but if I could not after the second chance, then that would be the final chance. It was a twist and I knew if I pushed the issue, I probably could have modified the agreement, but in the end, I decided that was acceptable.

So, a month later, after ninety days elapsed, it was time to attempt another orgasm and my last orgasm. As before, he had prepared some protocols for me to follow and I will copy the blog post I made about the evening here in its entirety:

> Last night was the end of my ninety days of chastity, and to say I was nervous is not even beginning to describe it. The thought of having my last orgasm, possibly ever, had been on my mind all day.
>
> I arrived at Sir's house a little early before he got home from work and prepared him a glass of bourbon before kneeling beside the door and waiting for him to arrive. After he got there and relaxed a bit, he had me follow him to the spare room where he again had me kneel before him while he explained his protocol for the night.
>
> He was granting me two chances to cum for the last time before going into permanent chastity. For this attempt, once my cage was removed, I would be presented with some numbing cream, two condoms, and a place to put my nub in an attempt to orgasm (the flashlight masturbation device as before). I have to say, looking down and seeing those keys for the first time in three months had me a little hard in the cage.
>
> I was reminded that since I decided to go into permanent chastity, if I were to be able to orgasm, that would be the last orgasm I would have in his service, at least. If, however, I was unable to orgasm within five minutes, I would be given an extension of fifteen days and I could come back and at that time, he would let me make one final attempt. However, on the second attempt, he would slightly reduce the restrictions. He would also be filming the attempt so I would have a record of my last orgasm if I had it.

I agreed and he unlocked my nub which began to precum as usual. Per Sir's instructions, I picked up the numbing cream and coated it until he told me to stop and then he handed me two condoms to put on.

As before, I was numb as hell and was sporting a rock-hard erection. Even Sir was impressed. I hoped that would bode well for me. He then started the timer and I got to work pounding away on the toy. However, I could already tell that it was too much numbing cream. I felt the buildup a few times, but it was just no use. He called time and I had to pull out. He had me remove the condom and clean up the remaining numbing cream and then kneel facing him.

I was reminded that I would be given another fifteen days of chastity and then I would be allowed one more chance to orgasm. So, I at least have that to look forward to.

After my attempt, Sir locked me up again and stuck a plug in my ass. He then had me follow him to the living room where he sat down on the couch to sip his bourbon and have a cigar. He directed me to get down on my knees and slowly work his cock over with my mouth. After about thirty minutes, he rewarded me with his seed down my gullet.

The next two weeks were intense for me. I knew I would not regret the decision I had made. I was ready, but I also really wanted one last normal orgasm unlocked, erect, and spurting. As the last day approached that this could happen, I was leaking precum like crazy and found it hard to pay attention at work at times.

Finally, February 2, 2016, came around. The last chance for me to have a normal orgasm as a male and the start of my permanent chastity. Here was the blog post I made:

I had my meeting with Sir tonight. He reminded me again that tonight was my final chance to orgasm before going into permanent chastity.

I was nervous and shaking a bit. He noted this and had me drop to my knees and suck on him a bit and let him fuck my face as well. After a bit, he had me rise and told me "it is time".

This time, I was told to coat my nub with a different type of lube. It was still desensitizing but was more fluid than the other lube we have used before. I think Sir was trying to give me a chance. Once I had a good coat, he handed me a towel and let it soak in. It felt numb but not as bad as the other stuff.

He reiterated, "this is your last chance boy" and then started the timer and announced, "five minutes starts now". I was surprised because I thought he would make me wear a condom again and he didn't make me use the toy. It was just me and my hand and my numb nub. I didn't waste time, though, and grabbed my nub and started jacking.

The lube started to penetrate my hands and they were going slightly numb, but I was determined to experience one last orgasm. I had to. It was like a mission. Sir counted off every fifteen seconds. After two minutes, I had to adjust a bit and try to get a better grip. My hands were numb, and my nub was numb, and I was panicking a bit.

I jacked furiously when at the three-minute thirty seconds mark and I could feel that feeling, that feeling of my balls wanting to release, but I just was not there. At four minutes thirty seconds, I concentrated and willed my nub would just blow. Please just blow. It was then I felt that feeling in my groin. Deep down I felt my balls start to swell and sure enough, I felt the surge of cum building ready to burst. Almost automatically, I looked into Sir's eyes and told him I was about to orgasm, and I wanted it to be my last normal orgasm as a male. I wanted to move into permanent chastity to service others.

As he looked at me and smiled, the cum came pouring out of my nub, and wave after wave of orgasm fell over me. I wasn't even fully hard and it wasn't the most mind-blowing of orgasms, but it was hard-fought and as I felt my nub pulse the last couple of times, it hit me what this meant, what I said, and what my future would be. I wasn't scared or frightened either. I was strangely content and happy.

Sir let me sit there for about a minute to have one last afterglow experience and he took a picture for me to remember the moment. But all good things must end, and he got me to my feet and after I cleaned up, he had me stand at attention with my hands behind my back.

He held my chastity device in his hand and told me that he was very proud of me and the decision I have made to go permanent and continue to learn and grow as a sub. He put some lube on my softened nub and I watched as he put on my device and locked it. He told me from now on whenever I needed the cage off to be cleaned, I would be blindfolded and bound. The intent was that I would never see myself out of chastity ever again to reinforce my decision and it was a condition that I agreed was a good one. He then spun me around and told me to bend over and he fucked a load into me as a reward.

That is how I started permanent chastity. I continued to see and service Sir for some time and moved to smaller cages over time as the tissues in my shaft atrophied from disuse, but eventually, he moved away and handed the keys back to me. I put them in a lockbox, and I have had trusted friends help me with cleaning the device every month, but I remained locked and chaste since that date in February 2016.

I have mentioned how your mind changes over time. For me, this is truly the case. I no longer want my cage removed and when it is for cleaning or for emergencies like when I had to go to the hospital for surgery, I long for it to be put back on. For those not into chastity and orgasm denial, this may seem weird or unhealthy, but for me, it is natural now and I intend to continue my permanent chastity journey for the foreseeable future. It has been over four and a half years since I last saw my nub unlocked and I had my last normal orgasm, and I don't know if there will be another.

Lessons Learned

While I have provided a summary of my experience and chastity journey, I often get asked about the lessons I have learned and the changes I have noticed in my body over time. The idea of long-term or even permanent chastity can be scary to most, something to read and fantasize about and/or something to aspire to depending on your role and interest. I will try to give some thoughts in these areas here.

Body Changes

When I first started in chastity and orgasm denial, I was above average in length. I am not trying to toot my own horn or anything, but this made me a bit concerned at first at not only getting the proper fit with a device but what effects in the short and long term this might have on my genitals. I do not regret anything I have done and would do the same thing again, but there are some things you should be prepared for if you are looking at moving into long-term or permanent chastity and orgasm denial.

The physical changes are noticeable. As I mentioned in chapter one, the body normally fills the erectile tissues of the penis every night several times a night to both exercise and keep things expanded and healthy. When you are in a chastity device, this swelling is greatly reduced. You can see atrophy of the tissues over time. Medical doctors have noted, and I mentioned previously, that this atrophy is reversible, but you can see shrinkage in the tissues of the shaft and a reduction in both girth and length over time.

The first change I noticed was girth. Within the first couple of months, I noticed that I did not fill the width of the cage I was using like I once did. The length was next and I have had to move to progressively smaller cages over time. For me, it has meant an adjustment about every year to a year and a half. I started in cages that were about 8.255 cm (3.25 in) in length and I am now in one that is 3.175 cm (1.25 in) in length. This is a reduction of about 38% in flaccid length and I would estimate about a similar reduction in flaccid girth.

I often get asked what the resulting atrophy looks like in the erect state, however, I do not get erect anymore since I am constantly in my cage. When the cage is removed for cleaning, I am always blindfolded since I don't want to see myself out of my cage. In the rare instances where I cannot find someone to help me clean the cage, I avoid looking at myself for the same reason. I have attempted erections at times while briefly uncaged, but I did not see it and there are no photos, so I cannot personally help here. However, anecdotally, I would expect a similar reduction in size for the erect state as well.

Again, this atrophy is reversible. If I were to stop chastity, I would expect a slow reversal in the appearance, but for me the smaller size is preferable. It means that I have a smaller cage and a smaller profile, and it is easier to wear under clothes and such as well.

Another change is how you groom your genital region. This is my personal preference, but I don't like going smooth. I have issues with ingrown hairs and pimples when I shave, and that is the last thing I want around a chastity cage. I do trim my groin area every couple of weeks, though. This is mainly to knock down the long hair, so it does not catch or pinch inside the chastity device I use. Different devices behave differently when you have even a small amount of hair, though, so your experience may differ from mine. I have found that I need to keep things at a shorter length when I am in plastic devices versus in those that are metal ones.

I have also noticed an increase in the production of precum. I have always produced a lot even before I was in chastity, but since I went permanent, the production has increased. I have also noticed that this flow rate tends to wax and wane during the month. I call them my "heat cycles" and when I am in a heavy flow period, I must be creative with my work clothes. I tend to go with two options. One is to use a sanitary pad that is normally used for women during their period. I use the small low-flow version they make for them and it works well in catching all the precum and keeping my pants dry. I have also used a sock to catch things on days that are not heavy flow. Again, your experience may differ, but be aware that an increase in precum production can often occur in chastity.

My doctor is aware of my permanent chastity. He is a gay doctor and I have been very open with him about it and wear my device as usual when I go for check-ups. He has been understanding and makes sure that I am taking care of myself and that there are no issues that I am having and that psychologically I am taking care of myself as well. We also check my hormone levels regularly since I suffer from low testosterone. I use Androgel cream on my thighs daily to boost this, but it is at a low level. I mainly want to keep my levels on the low end of normal to prevent the issues of bone loss and to prevent testicular atrophy as well. The last thing I need is my balls getting too small to hold my cage! I have opted to also keep the levels on the low end of normal so that I am not too horny and do not have a crazy high sex drive. As someone in permanent chastity and orgasm denial, that would not be a pleasant combination.

Personality Changes

Another question I often receive is how permanent chastity has changed either my attitude, personality, or psychology. I would say all three have been altered, but mainly because it was something I was striving to do. My goal in exploring chastity and denial was to put more of an emphasis on the pleasure and needs of the dominant I am with, not at the expense of my own, but to equally receive pleasure myself by doing so. In other words, I wanted to learn to get as much pleasure from serving the dominant as I got from pleasuring myself before.

I have mentioned in Chapter One that certain hormones are released when you achieve orgasm. This gives the male a warm and pleasant and relaxing feeling afterward. I have noticed that as I have gone for longer and longer periods in chastity and without orgasm, that my brain has compensated by letting me experience those feelings and I am assuming associated hormones when I bring a dominant to orgasm or hear them groan in pleasure. Indeed, it is a very fulfilling and pleasurable experience for me and has taken the place of any orgasm experience I used to have. Will the same happen for you? I do not know. However, others I have spoken with have had similar experiences, so it is something you can monitor and observe in your journey.

How I feel about my chastity device has changed over time as well. At first, it was something I was interested in and got a rush from wearing but was happy to take off and orgasm when I wanted or when the time was up. As I wore it for longer periods, however, I started to feel incomplete without it. I wanted it back on as soon as I could after a session was over and now, I feel like a part of my body is gone when it is taken off for cleaning. In a way, I guess I now see it as though it is an extension of my body and a symbol of my personality.

Finally, others have noted a definite change in my behavior to others. I am much more overtly subordinate even with my platonic friends. I tend to let others make decisions and I defer to people much more than I used to. This is probably because I am also interested in the dominant/subordinate dynamic and have trained myself to be more in deference to others, but I suspect the act of permanent chastity and orgasm denial also has played a role in this. I am perfectly happy with this change and welcome it, however.

One other change I have noticed is the need to seek out and interact with others, especially dominants. I write this text amid the Covid-19 pandemic and I realize that shortly, this will be behind us, but at the moment things are on lockdown and this has meant I have not had the chance to service or pleasure any dominants in over four months. This has been very tough for me and I have sought out those to talk to online and through social media outlets. It can be tough to find a good dominant that wants to take time out of their schedule to talk with a subordinate. Even in the best of times, they usually want physical pleasure and it is less about the daily or mundane interactions with us subs. But I have been fortunate to find a few, and I have a good number of friends that I can turn to talk to as well.

Communication is essential if you are going into long-term or permanent chastity and orgasm denial. I have mentioned this before, but it is probably the most essential aspect of chastity that you must make time for. Whether this is communication with your partner or partners, your dominant or with friends, you need to be able to discuss your feelings and have a place to find yourself. We are all social creatures and when you remove one aspect of your biological self, you need to replace it with something to compensate. Whether that be through physical and/or virtual interaction, make time for it and plan for it to be a part of your life as well.

CHAPTER FOUR

Appendix

Further Reading

When compiling this text, I asked for advice from others, questions they would like to see answered, and offered them the chance to provide me feedback, thoughts, and web links they found helpful in their chastity experiences. The following is a compilation of what I received and the names they chose to use.

Community Perspectives

Anonymous. Thanks for allowing me to add a little to your chastity book project. I wanted to pass along one thing that I have experienced and that is the need for a tease. I have had this issue with some of my keyholders in the past. If you have a keyholder that does not provide enough teasing or effective teasing, then I found that my overall arousal drops. I get bored and sometimes I lose interest. Granted, I only get into chastity periodically and am not as dedicated as you.

However, if someone has the same issue I have, then I think you need to talk to them and explain your issue. If they will not talk about or address the problem, then look for a different keyholder.

For those that self-lock and run into the problem of finding the stimulation that they need to keep their arousal at a high level, then I have some suggestions. Watching porn is always a good option or scrolling through some NSFW Twitter handles. You might also look at using a vibrator with your cage and do some edging. Anal play is another option as well. Whatever it is, find something to spice up your experience. Once boredom sets in, you are more likely to look to unlock.

John Doe. I wanted to pass along that many people wonder about the "chastity bump" or the outline of the device when you are wearing street clothes. Depending on the device you choose, it can be obvious you are wearing one, especially if you have tight clothes. I wear a device that has a profile that is noticeable at times, depending on the fit and style of the clothes I am wearing at the time.

Underwear is something you will want to reconsider. I find that boxers are more comfortable since they allow the device to move around, but they do not help with concealment and are not helpful if you are moving around a lot. Tight, brief-style underwear does a good job in hiding the device and keeping things in one place, but it can be more uncomfortable especially when sitting since it can put extra pressure on your balls. Jocks and specialty underwear meant to enhance or separate your package can often be a compromise, but again, it is going to show.

I've found almost all my pants and shorts telegraph that I'm wearing a device. Some just aren't as obvious about it. Many devices have a lower profile than others. In some cases, even if people notice the chastity bump, they may only assume you're a little better endowed than you are. At any rate, my last suggestion on clothing and concealment is to just get over it. It isn't possible to completely conceal most devices all the time. Sure, we all remember the embarrassment of the spontaneous boners when we were going through puberty. But chastity bumps aren't nearly that bad. Besides, we aren't going through puberty anymore. So, just let your freak flag fly. It's no one's business that you're wearing a chastity device. It's just another lifestyle choice, and it's perfectly legal.

76

G.B. I wanted to offer advice concerning your first night wearing a device. While I acclimated to sleeping in a chastity device fairly easily, I still remember the first night. I woke three times with a full tube, a tight scrotum, and a little burning sensation beneath the ring behind my ball sack. The tighter your sack at the beginning, the more you will probably experience that discomfort. The good news is the situation will eventually resolve itself if you wear a device long enough. Over time you find your scrotum will stretch and hang lower even when you're not wearing a device. Your body also adjusts to the sensations caused by the base ring when you have erections. I suppose your brain just gets used to it and stops sending you the pain signals.

Experiment with different sleep positions until you find the one that feels most comfortable for you. Intuitively, you might think sleeping on your back is the best. But I've found lying on my side, with my bottom leg more or less straight, and my top leg spread a little forward and bent at the knee works the best for me. My package rests on the bed between my legs and doesn't cause me any problems. After the first few nights, things will get better. After my first week, the nocturnal erections stopped waking me. Now I usually sleep fine.

Locked Flag

Twitter user Locked Morpheu has produced some great material on getting into chastity. His publication, Chastity Treaty, is listed in the reference section of this book and is a great read. He has worked to assist those exploring this fetish and even produced a flag that has been embraced by the chastity community.

The following is an excerpt in his own words from his text that describes how he came up with the flag design. I encourage those interested in chastity to use the flag where appropriate and to give credit and thanks to him for his creativity and efforts.

> Chastity is a fetish that is growing more and more around the world. Different from other fetishes, it is more personal and usually stays between the chaste and the keyholder and eventually internet photos. There isn't something that gathers

all chaste together as it happens with the Leather Community, even though some share the same fetish.

With the goal to unite all chastity adepts, I took the liberty of creating a flag to make us feel we are part of a collective. Flags always symbolized the union of people with something in common, that unite in one objective and a feeling of belonging. The Locked Flag concept came from the fact that no known fetish flag represents the chastity adepts because it is normal not to share this fetish with others even in the BDSM universe. That's why I wanted to do something specific that chaste can identify with.

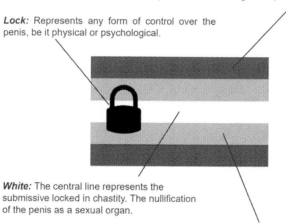

Dark Blue: The outside lines represent the masculinity perceived by society. All men are seeing like alphas at first glance.

Lock: Represents any form of control over the penis, be it physical or psychological.

White: The central line represents the submissive locked in chastity. The nullification of the penis as a sexual organ.

Light Blue: The second layer of lines show the true face of the chaste, when you can see the true nature of the locked man, inferior to other men.

The design came practically in a dream, at that moment when you are not fully awake, not fully asleep and the thoughts go unconscious through your mind. After trying different concepts and colors, the final flag ended up almost to the original concept.

The flag was first presented on May 10, 2019, in the Twitter account @lockedmorpheu and since then many adepts are using it in their profiles.

The flag and its meaning are all representatives of masculinity since today it is mostly used by males, been then heterosexual or homosexual.

The Locked Flag, like many other fetish flags, represents the adepts and the keyholders. It has been suggested a flag only for the keyholders or for the puppies that use chastity, but even though I had worked in a concept like this, I decided that making another flag would only divide the community and weaken the original goal of union. We want to spread this flag and make the chastity community stronger.

I want to thank the support I'm receiving from locked men and keyholders around the world.

- Locked Morpheu

Guides and FAQs

Becoming a Keyholder. For those that might be interested in holding the key for someone, Lock the Cock has a great article that discusses what to expect, helpful tips for success, and other advice. Read it here: https://bit.ly/306M1NQ

ChastiKey. This is the app that I mentioned that I and others have used before for self-locks with either someone online or for set periods. You will need a small lockbox with a code to make this work the best. This is a link to their FAQ if you want to learn more: https://chastikey.com/help/doku.php

Chastity 101. This is a great website made for males and females to get the ins and outs of chastity and answers to common questions. I have covered most in my book here, but it's a great resource as well: http://www.chastity101.com

FAQ of Chastity. This is a great article by Lovense that covers several questions from what is a chastity cage, to how you fit and wear them, to hygiene and care. It's a great read even if you have made it through my book: https://bit.ly/2Oh4TED

Flying and Chastity. I have flown several times with my chastity device. In the United States, they are considered "religious and cultural items" and are allowed. I have been waived on through and I have had pat-downs. Only once did I have to submit to a private screening, but that was at a small airport. If you want an account of what it is like, read this great article: https://bit.ly/30h0Hub

Pup Play and Chastity. Chastity and pup play often go hand in hand. If you want to learn more about how others are using chastity and orgasm denial in their lives in addition to pup play, this is a great article: https://bit.ly/3gPP0AZ

Why These Guys Put Their Dicks in Cages? There have been many articles about make chastity, especially as its popularity has risen in the past decade. Vice had a great article where they interviewed three men about their experiences, why they did it and how it changed their lives. It's a good read here: https://bit.ly/38WenP6

References

Adultsmart. (2018). An introduction to male chastity. Retrieved from https://malechastity.com.au/blog/an-introduction-into-male-chastity/

Barrett, K. (2018). What spending two weeks in a chastity device taught me about my sexuality and my marriage. Retrieved from https://www.independent.co.uk/voices/sex-locktober-chastity-belt-bdsm-marriage-relationship-sexuality-penis-a8600906.html

Devoted Lover. (2010). The key is on my nipple ring. Retrieved from https://devotedlvr.wordpress.com/2010/10/02/the-stages-of-chastity-dlmc/

Lock the Cock. (2018). How to measure for a male chastity device. Retrieved from https://lockthecock.com/blogs/chastity-fun/choosing-the-right-one

Masters, E. (2020). Cages, belts, and tubes. Retrieved from http://www.brassiered.com/tamingthecagedbeast/devices.html

Morpheu, L. (2020). Chastity Treaty. Retrieved from https://dombarbudo.com/wp-content/uploads/2019/07/Chastity-Treaty-English.pdf

Newland, J. (2019). Fetish illustrator. Retrieved from https://www.patreon.com/spacepupsilver

Savage, D. (2013). Savage love. Retrieved from https://www.thestranger.com/seattle/SavageLove?oid=16172896

ABOUT THE AUTHOR

L. D. Cub is an author of LGBT books and gay erotic fiction based in the United States. Most of his material involves the BDSM scene and chastity play and explores consensual relationships between adults over the age of 18. His stories have been published online and can also be purchased as an e-book or physical paperback as well. If you would like other formats or have feedback, please contact him at any time at the Twitter handle @LockedStories.

Made in the USA
Las Vegas, NV
30 January 2024

85094495R00050